Study Skills ESSENTIALS

Knowing how to play the game at school and university will help you to achieve exam success while having more fun than you might have imagined possible.

Drawing on the real-life experience of Oxford graduates this book reveals how to do really well at exams and coursework while actually still having a life.

Taking an approach that is both practical and realistic, author Patrick McMurray focuses on:

➢ Giving the examiners what they want to see
➢ Exam technique
➢ Getting organised to study effectively
➢ Coursework
➢ Essay-writing

This book is seriously useful. Reading it will significantly improve your study methods and exam technique, while allowing you time to have more fun as well.

First published in 2011 by Effective Study Skills Publications, 5 Demesne Manor, Holywood, BT18 9NW, Northern Ireland.

First edition 2011

ISBN 978-0-9568456-0-3

British Library Cataloguing-in-Publication Data: A catalogue record for this book is available from the British Library

Library of Congress Cataloguing-in-Publication Data: A catalogue record for this book is available from the Library of Congress

Printed and bound in the UK by Lightning Source UK, Chapter House, Pitfield, Kiln Farm, Milton Keynes, MK11 3LW.

Study Skills ESSENTIALS

Oxford graduates reveal their secrets

Contents

Introduction: How to do really well at exams

Knowing how to play the game at school and university allows you to achieve exam success while having more fun than you might have imagined possible.

Most people don't know how to play the game, for the simple reason that they have never been told the rules. Weirdly, exam technique isn't really taught in schools. Schools teach you what you need to know for exams. However they don't really teach you how to apply your knowledge in the exam, or how to approach a set of exams, or even how to approach a term's work in the first place. They don't teach you "how to do it". You're just kind of supposed to pick this up along the way.

This book is the missing piece of the jigsaw.

It draws on the practical experience of people who have done extremely well at school in real life. It outlines the techniques used by a wide range of Oxford graduates (plus a few others!) all of whom have sackloads of Grade As and First Class degrees behind them. They know "how to do it". And, after reading this book, so will you!

So how do you do really well at exams?

You find out what they want, and then you give it to them! Sounds simple doesn't it? Well that's because it is! Doing really well in exams is about playing the game. It's about jumping through the right hoops. You have to give them what they want to see. The problem is that most people don't really have a clear idea about what their examiners are looking for. But it's simply impossible to give them what they want if you don't know what that actually is! Read **Chapter 1** to find out how to make sure that you are aiming at the right target in the first place.

Don't waste work! 100% of the work that you do must be focussed on preparation for the actual exam or for coursework that counts towards the end result. Why? Because if you're not working then you can be out having fun, and having fun is really important if you want to do really well at exams (I think that you're going to find this book's new emphasis in this respect really quite refreshing). Read **Chapter 2** to find out how to get great results without having to lock yourself in the library.

Making the most of your day means that you have more free time at the end of it. Fitting in as much high-quality work as possible during the day means that there is more time for friends, family and doing other fun stuff (which is what we're really interested in). Read **Chapter 3** on "Organising your success" for tips on how to maximise free time, beat procrastination, and how to become one of those people who somehow get top grades without saying goodbye to their social lives.

Reading and taking notes is the bread and butter of student life - get this right and you will be off to a flying start. Read **Chapter 4** to revolutionise the way you approach any book or article.

Knowing how to write great essays comes in extremely useful in many different subjects. Read **Chapter 5** to discover a simple method that you can use again and again to produce one perfect essay after another.

Doing really well at coursework means that you will have less to do in the exam in order to get the grades you want. Read **Chapter 6** for tips on how to get high marks by giving them what they want, and so end up going into the exam with a vital head start. I've also added a section on how to do presentations – an increasingly common type of coursework, but one that many people haven't really come across before.

Chapters 7 and 8 draw on the experience of this book's contributors who provide specialist advice in the **particular subjects** that they studied – **Sciences** and **Languages** respectively. Turn straight to the sections that are relevant to you for subject-specific advice that has been proven to work in the real world.

You can only work properly if you're feeling fresh. Students who get the best grades often do so *because* they're the ones having the most fun. **Chapter 9** discusses the relationship between academic success and **making the very most of your time off.**

What is it that exams are really testing? Exams aren't just about *what you know* – they're also about *how you apply what you know* to the question that has been asked.   You can't apply what you know unless you actually genuinely **understand the material**. How do you go about doing this? Read **Chapter 10** to find out: the answer may be simpler than you think! This is, in fact, the most important chapter in the book. However I've left it until a bit later on because it's a slightly more abstract concept that might make more sense in the light of the earlier chapters.

No matter how good your notes are, if you can't remember them they are completely useless! **Chapter 11** outlines the most effective methods of **learning stuff**, so that there's absolutely no danger that you "go blank" when it matters most!

It's all about having the right **"exam technique"** – or so they say. But what does this actually mean? **Chapters 12, 13** and **14** show that there's really no mystery behind these magic words by considering what you need to do **before**, **during** and **after** the exam. In fact, this whole book is about exam technique: one of its fundamental messages is that doing really well at exams starts from the very first day of term.

How to use this book

Look at the beginnings and ends of each chapter: I've included sections on *"What's this chapter about?"* at the beginning of each chapter, and *"Essential points"* at the end. Use both of these to see if you're interested in the contents before diving in. In fact, if you're pushed for time you could probably get a lot of good ideas out of just reading the *"Essential points"* and leaving it at that.

Prioritise: Not all chapters are equally important – and this point applies to every book that you will ever read! If you are pushed for time, the absolutely essential sections to look at are Chapter 1 (Finding out what they want to see), Chapter 2 (How to never waste a moment's work) and Chapter 8 (Understanding). If you're studying a subject that involves writing essays then Chapter 5 could also be extremely useful.

Skipping around is fine: Don't feel that you have to read this book in the order that the chapters are set out in. While it would probably make most sense if you read it straight through, it's fine just to skip straight to the chapters that interest you most.

This isn't homework: If you are reading something and it isn't helping you then skip onto another section. If this – or any other book – is not helping you then just put it in the bin.

"University" points, and "School" points: Most of the material here applies both to school and to university, but I've also included certain points that only apply to one or the other. Skip over any sections that you feel are not relevant to you. Finally, given that at school you have "teachers" but at university you have "lecturers", I have decided to use the term "tutors" where the same point applies to both.

This stuff has taken me years to work out and I certainly haven't held anything back. I hope that you get a lot out of it.

1

Finding out what they want

What's this chapter about?

In order to play the game, you need to find out the rules. If you're going to give the examiner what they want to see, you need to find out what that is.

This chapter is about how to find out the rules of the game, so that the work you do is all going to contribute effectively towards your getting the grades you want. You need to make sure that your work is going to be pointing in the right direction.

How do you find out what they want to see? You do it by getting the most out of your relationship with the person teaching you, by using past papers correctly (not just before the exams!), by making smart use of the syllabus and the internet, and by being willing to learn from the other students around you.

More fundamentally, however, this chapter is about taking control of your own studies, and actively finding out for yourself what's required, so that you can get the results you need.

Congratulations

The very fact that you are reading this book shows that you have got the right attitude towards your studies. You're taking responsibility for getting the grades that you want. Reading books like this is part of the process required to actually make it happen. You're not sitting passively, hoping that your teacher or lecturer will get you the results that you need.

Taking this sort of very active approach to your studies is absolutely central to the success you will achieve. You're thinking for yourself and taking the initiative. On the basis of the simple fact that you are reading this, I believe that you are more likely to succeed than other students.

Why is it so important to find out what they want?

I've put this as the very first chapter in the book for a reason. The entire philosophy of this book is that you have to play the game – that you have to give them what they want to see. But here's the point: you can only give them what they want, if you actually know what it is that they want. You're only likely to hit a target if you have a good idea where it actually is.

Most students don't really have a clear idea about what their examiners want to see. But how can you possibly give them what they want to see, if you don't know what that is?

Finding out what they want underpins the entirety of the work that you should be doing as a student. First you find out what they want. Then you can target and focus your work on giving it to them. You can only target your work if you know what they want to see in the first place. You need to know where the target is.

This is the first thing that you need to do when you're approaching a new course. You need to make sure that you're heading towards the target from the very first few weeks.

Crucially: Who are we trying to impress here?

What matters is your end result, and so the people we are trying to impress are the people who are marking the work that directly counts towards this end result.

If the end result is decided by an exam, then we will be trying to impress the examiner.   Ultimately the person you really need to impress is someone you may never meet: the examiner. At school you won't know who your examiner is, but at university it will often be the same person who gives your lectures and classes on that subject. The approach in this book is all about giving the examiner what he or she wants to see. It's about playing the game, and jumping through the right hoops just the way the examiner wants you to.

If there is a coursework component then you will also be trying to impress the person who is marking that coursework, and that person is usually your teacher or lecturer. Read Chapter 6 to find out how to get great marks in coursework, and so put yourself in the very best position possible for when you are going into the exam.

This definitely isn't about being "teacher's pet": The approach of this book is not just about "doing what your teacher says". It's about thinking for yourself, and making sure that you get the grades you want. However creating a good relationship with the person teaching you can help put you in the best position possible for when you sit down in the examination hall. Reading the rest of this chapter will show you how to do this.

Working *with* the person teaching you: how to get the most from this relationship

While it's the examiner who you are trying to impress, the person teaching you is the most important person in helping you to find out what the examiner wants and likes to see.

There are some important limitations here:

- **Some teachers and lecturers are much better than others:** There is a wide range of ability in teaching, just as there will be in any other job.
- **You're part of a class:** Your teacher or lecturer generally interacts with you as part of a class (again with a wide variety of abilities), and so the amount of individualised input they can give you will be limited.

These limitations mean that there is only so much you can realistically expect your teacher or tutor to be able to do. The person teaching you is an important ingredient in your academic success, but there are many other ingredients in this recipe.

At university you will have more freedom and so will be expected to take more responsibility and initiative for directing your own learning.

If you want to be successful, you have to come to appreciate that learning is not just about teacher you telling you exactly what to do and then you going off and doing it. There's more to it than that. You have to work out a lot for yourself. Matt

Reading books like this shows that you have switched your brain to "ON", and that you are taking responsibility to make sure that you get the grades you want.

Your attitude to the person teaching you needs to be this: You want to squeeze every last drop of useful information and insight out of this relationship. The more understanding you gain from the person teaching you, the less work you will have to do yourself, and the better you will do in the exam. Your tutor is one of the most valuable resources you have.

Here is how to make the most out of this important relationship:

- **LISTEN:** Pay close attention to what your tutor is saying in class. Many tutors are excellent, and have years of experience seeing people both succeed and fail in their particular subject.

  I went and asked questions, and never stopped asking questions. And I asked people for help. That's how I got a First. Sunita

- **ASK SPECIFIC QUESTIONS:** If you don't understand something then take the time to ask your teacher about it after class. Ask your tutor about what sorts of different questions might be asked on the particular topic that you are studying (what different angles might an examiner take?). One on one input can be extremely useful, yet many students don't make the most of this valuable resource. If your particular tutor isn't explaining something clearly or in a way you understand ask a different teacher in the same subject.

- **ASK GENERAL QUESTIONS:** Get an overview of where the course is heading. Ask your tutor directly about the sort of skills and aptitudes you will need to succeed in their particular subject. Get them talking by asking questions like "where do most students struggle with this subject?", or "where do students often have problems in the exam with this subject?". Exams are usually marked by tutors during their summer holidays. It's likely that your tutors will have done quite a bit of marking themselves. They therefore will know about the marking criteria used by the exam boards. In other words, they know what the examiner is looking out for. You just have to ask them what this is!

Working *with* your teacher: feedback & how to get it

What's feedback? Getting feedback is when you discuss your work with your tutor, and you get some advice as to how you might improve and get a better mark.

Benefit from your teacher's experience: Your tutor will probably have years of experience of seeing students doing the particular course that they are teaching. Make sure that you benefit from this, so that you can improve your own performance.

Taking the time: The vast majority of students don't bother doing this. So you can gain a big advantage over other students who don't know or are too lazy to take this step.

Here is how to do it:

- **Get as much detail as you can:** If a tutor says that your essay was "pretty good", don't just say "thanks". Ask for specific suggestions on how you could have done it better. The key question is this: "how could I have got a better mark?" Even if you have done well there will always be something that you could adjust that will squeeze you out an extra mark or two. Even if you got a really good mark, you might be surprised at how much room there is to improve. This is particularly the case in "Arts" subjects where typically a First class mark will be about 70%. Ask them how you could have got 80% (a *high* First).

- **Get feedback regularly:** Try to get solid feedback on pretty much every substantial piece of work that you hand in. If you are going to improve, you need to know where you are going wrong!

- **At university** many lecturers have **"office hours"** when any of their students can come and ask them questions about their lectures or tutorials.

  Why it's useful: "Office Hours" are a golden opportunity to find out what your lecturer wants to see, and to get some valuable one-on-one tuition. This is all the more important given that at university your lecturer is also likely to be your examiner. Your tutor will quite likely want to help you because your success will reflect well on them.

  How to make the most of "office hours": Ask your tutor what they think makes a good essay (etc) in the subject that you're doing. Ask them about common mistakes that they see students making. Take a list of questions to make sure that you get the most out of the experience, and make sure that they're good ones so that your tutor doesn't feel that you are wasting their time. It might be worth emailing them these questions in advance so that they have a time to think about them. Write down anything useful they say and add it to your notes. Above all, don't be embarrassed at going to see them – this is what you are paying your fees for!

- **Good feedback will be phrased positively:** So, someone who is skilled in giving feedback will say "I think one area you could very usefully work at is X", rather than "You're a weak student because you never get X right". Good feedback will include some encouragement as well as pointers that you can learn from. Feedback is often not communicated particularly well. It's vital that you make the most of the content of what is being said, even if the packaging leaves something to be desired.

Past papers: know your enemy

Thinking about what questions might come up just a few days before the exam is FAR too late and is COMPLETELY STUPID. Start thinking about what you are working towards right from the very beginning of the course. Sunita

When's the first time you see an examination paper? For many people, the first time they see an exam paper is sitting in the hall on the day of the exam.

The normal approach: People often think that past papers should be used towards the end of the revision process, to help with preparation for exam day itself. This is definitely not a bad idea, and I will discuss it more on p 206.

What you need to do: Get your hands on the past papers not towards the end of your revision process, but **on the very first day that you start studying for that particular subject**.

Know your enemy: Know what you are working towards, and what it is that you will have to do battle with.

Psychologically, going through the past papers at the beginning of the course will remind you to focus your efforts completely on the exam that will be coming at the end.

Here is what to look for:

* **Content of the questions:** Make a list of which topics come up in each past paper so that you can see which topics come up year after year. Later, when revising, you can look more closely at the wording of the questions to see the particular angles that the examiner is keen to focus on.

- **Type of questions:** Is it essays or source questions? Is it problem questions? Whichever type of questions the exam contains, you need to get good at them. So, for example: if you have to answer a source question and have not done many of these before, then you will have to acquire the relevant techniques. If it is a science exam but there is an essay component then you will have to learn how to write an essay. You need to get good at ALL the different components of the exam, not just the ones you are naturally good at or enjoy the most!

- **Where the marks are:** Take language exams as an example - here 50% of the mark is frequently allocated on the basis of the listening and speaking components. However students often practise these skills a lot less than their reading and writing in the foreign language. So extra work developing speaking and listening skills might well go a long way (See Chapter 8).

Examiners' Reports: Straight from the horse's mouth

What are Examiners' Reports? Examiners often actually publish their thoughts indicating what they like to see, and outlining the ways in which students often fail to deliver this. Think of Examiners' Reports as being like a brick wall that examiners bash their heads off, as students make the same mistakes year after year.

Here are some examples taken from some reports on a set of English Literature exams:

*"As with the other Shakespeare plays this year, candidates were more prepared to work with the **language** of the extract, which is very positive indeed"*

*"The better responses used the **stage directions** to good effect, right up to the end of the extract"*

*"In the unseen poem, the best candidates worked from the most obvious meaning of the words on the page and **considered the way that those words were used**... however some ignored the poem's **conclusion**, which, as with all texts, is never a good idea. Many went further and explored the **imagery and its significance**"*

As you can see, Examiner's Reports can contain really useful stuff. Take the opportunity they offer to learn from other people's mistakes.

Where do you get Examiner's Reports from?

- Your teacher or lecturer: It is highly likely that he or she has a copy of these reports in their filing cabinet. Amazingly tutors usually don't share these with their students, when in actual fact they should be stapling them to each student's forehead. Make sure you ask your tutor for a copy.
- Your school or university's Head of Department in that subject.
- The exam board's website.
- The internet: If you are studying *Romeo and Juliet* at GCSE, for example, just Google the name of the play along with "Examiners Reports'". It doesn't particularly matter if you find material from your specific exam board or from another one.

When? As with past papers, get your hands on the Examiners' Reports right at the beginning of the year. **Why?** Well, there is no point finding out what they want a few days before the exam when it is too late to do that much about it.

The Curriculum: what you need to know

What is "the Curriculum", exactly?

- It's the list of stuff that could come up in the exam.
- Each examination board will produce a copy of this, as a guide for teachers in schools. The teacher does not have to teach you the whole curriculum, as (depending on the subject) it may be possible

to be well-prepared for the exam without having covered the whole curriculum.

How is it useful?

- **There it is in black and white:** This is the exam board telling you clearly and simply about the sort of stuff that you need to know.
- **It's a good overview** of where you are headed with the course. This means that, even in the early stages, you have a good idea of where what you are learning fits into the bigger picture of the course.
- **It helps you decide which work is really important:** Work is only important if it directly impacts on the grade that you are ultimately awarded. Some tutors like to cover other ground as well, in order to "practise" doing the proper work.
- **So, for example:** In English Literature some teachers will go through *Macbeth* with you in preparation for reading *Hamlet* – the play that is actually on the exam. But if you know that *Macbeth* is not actually going to be on the exam, then you should give it less work than you will be doing for the play that is actually on the exam. See Chapter 2 on "How to never waste a moment's work" for ideas on how focussing your work can save you time.

Learning from other students

Find someone who has either done very well, or who is doing very well, and ask them their advice. They will be flattered and you can definitely pick up some brilliant tips.

Ask them about:

- General approach
- Having a look at their work if they are getting better marks than you.
- Choice of subjects for the following year. They might know which are the good teachers and which it is better to avoid.
- They may even be kind enough to lend you a few of their notes, which might come in very handy indeed.

The best students are always getting better: Even if you are already one of the top people in your year, there will definitely be things that you can learn from other people who are also doing really well at exams. It could really be worth having a few chats with them about how *they* do it, because chances are they will be doing it a little differently to you.

Google around for tips in your particular subject

Example: If you Google for "study tips Maths" you will get some really useful results, especially if you are prepared to dig deep and look through three or four pages of search results.

Whatever subject you're doing take half an hour to Google around and to see what you can find. It could significantly improve how you approach your subject.

There will be a lot of nonsense on the internet, of course: Try to focus on contributions from people teaching at universities who are more likely to know what they are talking about.

New types of question: The same point applies if you are struggling with a new type of question that you aren't quite sure how to do. If you Google "history source question technique" you'll probably get some extremely useful advice.

More advanced search techniques on Google: Bear in mind that there are more precise ways of searching for things on Google. For example, if you search for jaguar – cars (that's a minus sign there) you'll get results that find jaguars of the animal variety but not of the car variety. There are a few other useful tricks like this that you can find under "basic search help" – Google it!

Essential points:

✓ You can only give them what they want once you have found out what this actually is.

✓ There's only one person who can make sure you will get the grades you want – you.

✓ The person you're trying to impress is the examiner, who may or may not be your tutor.

✓ Your tutor is the best resource you have to find out what the examiner wants.

✓ Past papers should be used at the very beginning of the course, as well as towards the end.

✓ Ask other students about how they are getting good marks.

✓ Google around to find tips for your particular subject.

2

Never waste a moment's work

What's this chapter about?

This chapter is about working effectively. I know that this sounds incredibly boring, but trust me, I've written this chapter for the very best of reasons. Getting more work done in less time means that you will have the opportunity to spend more time with friends and family, while still having a good day when you get your results.

Doing work takes quite a lot of effort, so you need to make it really count. This chapter will tell you how.

The issues covered are as follows:

> ➢ the importance of taking time off
> ➢ the type of work you should focus on
> ➢ length of work sessions and breaks
> ➢ using a computer to save you time

Here's the good news

This book is on your side: *I want you to get the best possible results you can, but to have plenty of time for spending time with your friends and generally chilling out.*

I believe that having fun and enjoying a balanced lifestyle is really, really, important.

More than that, relaxing properly is one of the key things that you MUST do if you want to get excellent results. You can only study properly if you're fresh. You'll only be fresh if you've had some good time off enjoying yourself – that's common sense.

I think that you'll find this book's take on this issue to be really quite refreshing. I have a very positive attitude towards taking breaks, towards taking time off, and to generally having as much fun as possible.

Here's the maybe slightly less good news

If you want to get excellent results, you're going to have to do really quite a lot of work. Unfortunately that's common sense too.

There's no "magic bullet": Funnily enough, people who do loads of work tend to do really well. When I was at Oxford the people who were in the library from day one all got the best marks.

Before writing this book, the very first friend I asked for his tips just laughed and said:

```
Well, doing some work would probably be a good
start.   The  best  study  tip  is  to  actually
study.   The  more  you  study  and  the  more  you
learn, the better you'll do, it's as simple as
that.   Will
```

However my aim in this book is to show you how to get good grades while still having fun. *Here's how to do it:*

Never, ever, waste a minute's work

The only work that matters is work that counts directly towards the result that you get at the end of the year. This will either be (1) work that will contribute directly towards your performance in the exam, or (2) coursework that counts towards the end result.

So every minute's work that you do has to directly contribute towards your performance on the day of the exam, or to coursework that counts towards your final mark.

You need to apply this policy from the very first day of the course.

But what if a piece of work doesn't count towards my final mark?

Prioritisation is the name of the game: If a piece of work doesn't count towards your final mark then doing it is pretty much a waste of time. If you can get away with it then simply don't do that piece of work. If you can't get away without doing it, then do enough to get by but no more than that. Give it the bare minimum of effort and waste as little time as possible on it. You need to be spending your time on work that actually counts.

DANGER: Don't get on the wrong side of a tutor who will be marking work that actually counts towards your end result, or from whom you are likely to need a reference in future.

EXAMPLE - the class test:

- **The situation:** So, say you have a class test, which does not count towards your main exam.
- **Many people think:** "I know it's just a class test so the result doesn't really count for anything. But I suppose I ought to do a bit of work for it. I'll just start preparing a couple of days before. That should be enough for me to get by."
- **What you should think:** Yes, the actual result that you get in this test doesn't matter at all. However preparing for the test is a great opportunity to get your notes in order, notes that you can use when it is time to revise for the real exam.
- **What not to do:** Don't waste time preparing notes for a class test if they are not going to be of good enough quality to use for the real thing. Equally, don't waste time learning your notes if they are not going to be the notes that you use for the real thing. There is no point going to quite a bit of effort to compile some rubbish notes and to half-learn them. This is wasted work.
- **What to do:** Spend time getting your notes really good, and understanding the work properly. Do work that will be useful for the proper exam in six months time.

- **What I'm not saying:** The message here is not "don't do any work for the class test". What I'm saying is: preparation for the real exam is your number one priority, so make sure the work you do for class tests contributes solidly towards this more important objective.
- **Outcomes:** Working on your "proper" notes may mean that you don't have enough time to cram for the class test, and so do less well in the class test than you might have done. That's ok. It's your preparation for the exam that matters.

So here's the flip side: If work is useful for the exam, then do it properly - give it some really serious and proper effort. There is only going to be a certain amount of work that you are going to be able and willing to do, so make it really count.

Who decides whether work is useful or not? You do. When a teacher or lecturer sets a bit of work, they won't ever say "this isn't that relevant to the exam, so don't bother too much about it" or "just dash this off – don't waste too much time on it". They don't really tell you whether a particular piece of work is important or not. Switch brain to "ON" and make these decisions for yourself.

Working effectively

Working effectively (1): Work in short bursts

MYTH: Many people think that to do really well at exams you have to spend crazy amounts of time slumped over your desk, match-sticks propping up your eyelids – they think that you really have to SUFFER.

MYTH: It's not an endurance battle against yourself. Just going through the motions is pointless and a waste of time. Don't confuse the effort you are making with the results that you likely to get. You don't get graded on how many hours you study - you get graded on what you learn and understand, and on how well this allows you to perform in the exam.

REALITY: *Most of your work sessions should last no longer than about 40 minutes.*

Intense, high quality work is key: Working smart, with your brain switched to "ON", and with the aim of achieving genuine understanding of the material at hand. This will involve actually thinking a lot, and thinking is hard work.

Psychological studies back this up: Humans generally can't concentrate on something for more than about 30-40 minutes. In fact, at Oxford some of the psychology lecturers give everyone a short break half-way through the lecture so that they can come back fresh for the second half. Given that the fact that we can only concentrate for 30-40 minutes is naturally the case, is really important that we work *with* nature and not against it.

Some sessions should in fact be shorter than 40 minutes: If you are doing particularly intense work, such as learning, then 25 minutes per session could be enough. It's all about what works best for you as an individual. If you're not concentrating properly then there's no point in being there.

Some sessions can be longer: If you are totally "in the zone" then just run with it and keep working. Sometimes when you are writing an essay, for example, it all just comes together and starts to flow. Don't stop! Keep cranking it out until you start to feel yourself getting stale.

Don't kid yourself that you are working if you are not! Just because you are sitting at your desk doesn't mean that you are achieving anything. Just because you "pulled an all-nighter" doesn't mean that you actually got more than an hour and a half's work done after the clock had struck midnight.

Working effectively (2): Length of breaks

What are we trying to achieve here? The aim of the game is that of genuinely understanding the work, so that you can apply it in the exam. This requires high levels of concentration. There is no point trying to understand work properly if you are too tired or distracted to focus properly.

Boredom is the enemy: If you aren't pretty fresh your brain will pretty much shut down, and you will be left just going through the motions, which is a pointless waste of time.

Therefore, when you are taking a break, take as long as you need so that you come back fresh. How long this takes depends on you as an individual.

There is no such thing as the five minute break: Be honest with yourself. There is no point in saying "oh I'll just take five minutes", but then spending the next ten minutes guiltily conning yourself saying "well that can't be more than five minutes". Give yourself at least 10 minutes break – and guilt-free, you've earned it!

Next steps: The last thing you should do before taking your break is to figure out what's the next work you need to do on that topic. Writing this down on a Post-it note before heading off to relax will mean that you aren't thinking about it when you are supposed to be recharging your batteries. You should also do this if you aren't going to be coming back to that piece of work for a day or two.

What should you do during your break? Don't just get tired and then slide into checking something on the internet. Decide to take a proper break and make the most of it.

Make it a definite break:

- Get away from your desk.
- Get outside. The fresh air will help you feel more awake.
- Do some physical activity like chucking a ball around.

- Phone a friend, if you can do this without kissing goodbye to the next hour and a half.
- Have a shower.

Be honest with yourself: When thinking about how much work you have done, be honest! If you do a 45 minute session and then have a 15 minute break don't kid yourself into thinking that you have in fact done an hour's work.

Working effectively (3): How much work should I aim to do in a day?

5 hours of solid work per day was my target in the run-up to exams, on days when I wasn't at school. I measured the work strictly, and didn't count breaks at all. Doesn't sound that much? Maybe not. But remember the emphasis is on doing high quality work, which is high-intensity and therefore fairly demanding.

Keep your work sessions short: You shouldn't work for more than about two and a half hours at a stretch without taking a really good long proper break of at least an hour, preferably more. As always our goal here is to come back fresh and ready to do some serious work. Spending 4 hours at a stretch just sitting at your desk is simply not going to be productive.

Universities often suggest that their students should be doing about 40 hours of study per week. Frankly, I think that this is both unrealistic and unnecessary. If you are doing intellectual work properly it will be very demanding. Moreover, if you are working efficiently and using the techniques outlined in this book, I think that you can work much less than 40 hours a week and still get the top grades.

How to get work done

- **Targets:** Set yourself a regular goal each day. If you keep hitting this target your total hours will start to mount up.
- **Habits:** Humans are creatures of habit. **Create a routine** that maximises the total number of hours that you are able to spend preparing for the exam.
- **Run with it:** Some days you will just feel "in the groove" and will just be able to keep on working. Just run with it! Particularly in the build-up to exams you may "feel the fear" and find yourself putting in 12 hour days, wishing that there were more hours in the day! When the fear arrives, use it.
- **Get work for free:** Any time you feel even vaguely inclined to do some work just go ahead and do it. In a sense you get this work "for free" in that you are not having to force yourself to do it. If you are feeling the urge to work, then make the most of it!
- **Avoid drift:** Sometimes towards the end of the day you might find yourself at your desk but not really concentrating, almost just waiting for your session to end, maybe starting to surf the internet a little. Don't kid yourself that you're working - this is a complete waste of time.
- **Avoid "fake work":** Either work, and work properly, or quit and go and have some fun. Don't get stuck half way, doing neither one thing nor the other. There's no point in thinking "look busy! the boss is coming!" – YOU'RE THE BOSS!

It is very easy to convince yourself that you are studying when you really aren't. Matt

- **Manage yourself:** Calculate how much work you can realistically get out of yourself in a day. Plan to do this and then quit. **KNOW YOURSELF**. Notice how many hours you tend to work before you burn out and become unproductive. This will allow you to make a guilt-free decision to stop working for the day, and to do so at the right time.
- **Once you're done, you're done:** Once you've stopped working for the day, put it out of your mind completely. Take a definite decision that

you are finished for the day, write down what you need to do next, then quit.

- **Make the most of your mornings:** The morning can be a great time to get some work out of the way. Do the subjects that you like the least or that require more thinking earliest in the morning, when you are at your freshest. Sneaking in an hour before nine or ten o'clock will get your day off to a flying start, and almost guarantee that it is fairly productive.

- **"All-nighters" don't work:** Very few people work effectively at night. Don't kid yourself that you are really putting in the hard yards just because you are spending ten hours in a row at your desk. In reality – and as someone who's been there many times – I can tell you that you're probably achieving very little. It's just not natural to be up at 3.45 am, and it totally wipes out the next day as well.

- **Don't burn out:** Too much work is counter-productive and unsustainable. Having a balanced lifestyle will help to prevent this.

Work consistently - be a worker not a slacker

Work consistently: You cannot afford weeks during term where you are not really doing that much work. Getting into the habit and routine of working is essential if you want good results. Quantity really matters. People who do a lot of work tend to do well, it's that simple. That's why the mode you generally need to be in is "working", not "slacking".

Keep chipping away: Understanding arrives gradually and it takes time. Your brain needs time for new concepts to sink in.

DANGER: The classic mistake is only to really start working in the run-up to the exam. However, if you play it this way, you simply cannot hope to compete with people who have been working solidly from day one. You can only do so much in a day so need to work consistently so that work can build up.

One guy I knew did next to nothing for two and a bit years, but then spent 4 months grinding out sixteen hour days in the library and did fine in the end. That said, another guy I know did next to nothing for two and a bit years, and kept saying that "the big push" was just around the corner. It never happened...he flunked. Johnny

The trick is to *be* one of those people who have been working pretty solidly from day one. I'd love to be able to tell you that there's a way of getting great results on the basis of very little work, but there simply isn't.

When should I start to revise? There should be no real distinction between your "ordinary" work during term and your "revision". Both kinds of work are headed towards the same goal – that of performing well in the exams.

CLASSIC MISTAKE: So often people just scrape by through the term and then begin their "revision" far, far too late. In fact, it's not revision, because it's actually them having to do and to try to understand the work properly for the very first time. Inevitably they end up not having time to understand it, and – crucially – not having time to actually learn it (See Chapter 11).

Motivation

Only you know whether or not you're motivated to do the work necessary to fulfil your potential.

The very fact you are reading this book suggests that you might well agree with the following:

Working hard at school often leads to a good job with good pay. Time spent now can have big dividends down the line. I always felt if someone had told me the bare facts from day one I would have been more inclined to change my own destiny with some actual work. The hours you work at school or university will seem like nothing if you're stranded in a dead end job. Trev

Messages to keep you motivated: Why not put a **picture beside your desk** of something that will motivate you when the going gets tough? So if you are studying hard because you want to be a doctor then why not pin up a picture from some medical show off the television? If you want to make a lot of money then put up a picture to remind you of the lifestyle that all this hard work will hopefully allow you to enjoy.

Use the power of your imagination: The imagination is an extremely powerful tool when it comes to motivation. It exerts its power through the pictures and stories in our minds. Imagine yourself as the doctor arriving on the scene, knowing exactly what to do, and then rewarding yourself with a nice meal out at the end of the week. Watch TV shows or read internet sites that relate to the direction that you want to take your life in, and so will remind you of the reasons that you're doing all this hard work.

Put a Post-it note with a message to yourself on the wall beside your desk or on your computer screen, using its "Post-it note" function. Write whatever it takes to encourage you to focus just that little bit harder. Or why not pin up some **good exam results** that you got in the past to boost your confidence?

Focus: How to avoid distraction

What's the aim here? When you are working, you need to be working. You need to be actively thinking about and seriously engaging with the material in a genuine effort to understand it.

Computers can save you a lot of time, but they can also waste a lot of time:

- **Social networking sites** can be a big problem here. Many people (including myself) spend an absolutely incredible amount of time checking these sites. The time spent doing this really adds up hugely. One idea of limiting the amount of time doing this is to only check these sites at certain times during the day. Another idea is to only accept the "friend requests" of people that you are genuinely close friends with. The most extreme option, of course, would be to delete membership of these sites completely.

- **Instant messaging:** This is perhaps the worst of the lot, because instant messages can pop up at any time.

- **Don't become an internet zombie:** Whatever you do, don't just start aimlessly surfing the internet while feeling guilty about it. We've all been there, of course. But it's not exactly a great way of recharging your batteries. The internet is incredibly useful but is also the biggest time-sucker ever. If you must look at something online try to do it in a different room so that it seems like more of a break.

- **Don't flick between your work and the internet:** The danger is that you spend your time flicking between doing work and looking at other stuff. We've all done it. The problem is that this means the work done is of extremely low quality. To reduce temptation you can shut down all internet screens so that you aren't tempted to flick between your work and the net. You could also delete any "shortcuts" to the internet that exist on your computer. Taking these steps makes looking at the internet a more active choice, rather than something you just drift into because you're losing concentration.

Music vs the sound of silence

- **A help or a hindrance?** Lyrics and radio babble can be very distracting. But some music can in fact be a useful tool for getting you "in the zone".

- **What's your "game song"?** Boxers sometimes have "game songs" that they listen to in order to get them in the mood. Putting on some rock music or some dance music can really help the work along.

- **"White noise"** is the sound of waterfalls or raindrops and can be used to block out the sound of distractions. You can find it for free on the internet.

- **Ear plugs** can also come in very handy, both for revision and for promoting a good night's sleep. The foam ones work best.

Use the right tools: Get a computer and learn how to use it

This is one of the most important pieces of advice in this book.

If at all possible, it is absolutely essential that you:

- Get your hands on a computer
- Learn how to type
- Learn how to use Microsoft Word® or equivalent

If you don't already have a computer, then get one if at all possible.

Why? Well, you should get one because...

* Using a computer will save you absolutely enormous amounts of time*

How? Here are just some of the things that you can do on a computer that will save you absolutely shed-loads of time:

- **"Cut and paste":** These are the magic words that you will come to know and love. They refer to a function of Microsoft Word® that saves you writing things out again and again. You just have to type it out once, and then you can copy and paste it as many times as you like. "Cut and paste" makes it amazingly easy to create summary notes to revise from. You can put together notes in a few minutes that would otherwise have taken you literally hours to create. Note that there are some useful shortcuts in Microsoft Word® – e.g. Copy is (Control + C), Cut is (Control + X), Paste is (Control + V).
- **"Find and replace" is another extremely useful function:** Rather than typing out "Thucydides" every time, just type T and then just Control + F to replace your abbreviation with the full word.
- **Make your text more attractive:** Making your text bold (Control + B), italicised (Control + I) or underlining it (Control + U) can make it easier to read.

Impression makes a big difference: Coursework looks a lot better when you have typed it out on the computer. For some reason a piece of typed work just looks more impressive, more "proper", as well as being easier to read. The mere fact that you have done the work on the computer will probably get you a slightly higher mark.

Computers: Here is what you need to do

Get the basic model: You don't need anything fancy. What you need for work is word-processing - meaning the ability to create and to write documents - and this is a very basic computer function. Widescreen computers can be particularly good because you can have two documents open and side-by-side, allowing you to easily create notes by which cutting and pasting from one document to the other (however widescreen laptops will be heavier).

Microsoft Word® is the software that you need: This is the most commonly used word-processing package (similar programmes are available!). As a student you should be able to get software cheaper than otherwise, so look into this (Google is your friend here).

Anti-virus software is an absolute must: If a virus gets into your computer you can lose a lot of work which is a complete disaster. Make sure that the software you choose is regularly updated. At the time of writing AVG offers free antivirus protection.

Backing up your work, either using an external hard-drive or online is also a complete must, for the same reasons. You must have a copy of your key documents saved somewhere other than on your computer. Computers sometimes just stop working, so take precautions.

Programmes that allow you to make the most of your computer

Microsoft Word® is user-friendly and extremely easy to use after a bit of practice. Note that some free programmes like OpenOffice® might also give you what you need.

- **What you need to know:** The functions that you actually need to use within Microsoft Word® are extremely basic. Don't worry about the fancy stuff, just concentrate on being able to create and save documents that you will need to be able to do work and revise for school. It also has a spell-check, which is useful. Make sure that it is set to the correct version of English (i.e. UK or American).
- **How to learn how to use it:** Get someone who knows how to use it to show you how. Alternatively there will be good tutorial videos if you search on YouTube (although make sure that they are tutorials on the particular version of word that you actually have). Write down their instructions so that you can repeat them yourself.
- **Organising your files on the computer:** Create a separate file for each subject that you are studying, with sub-files for each topic or week's work. If your computer files are a mess then it can be just as frustrating as if your paper files are in a mess, believe me.

Microsoft PowerPoint® allows you to quickly create presentations. It allows you to create slides and then you can move from one slide to another in your presentation. Learn how to use it if you get the chance. When you get to university and the world of work you will be expected to know how to do this. Pick up PowerPoint by playing around with it yourself, by asking someone to give you a quick lesson, and by learning from instructional videos on YouTube.

Microsoft Excel®: This is the Microsoft's "numbers" programme. Excel® allows you to manipulate numerical material, and to create amazing graphs and other visual representations. If you are doing Maths or science you will definitely be encountering it in the near future. So you may as well get up to speed as early as possible, and be able to make use of it to improve your work and to save you time.

Learn how to type! Seriously!

Being able to use the computer is really important, and so knowing how to type is also majorly important.

Learn how to type – this is one of the very most important pieces of advice in this book

Why bother? If you don't know how to type properly, you will not be making the most of what your computer has to offer, and will be wasting absolutely loads of time.

Typing is one of the most useful skills that you will ever learn. Again, when you are at university or in the world of work you will totally be expected to know how to do this. Just learn how to do it now! **It will save you a TON of time.**

You don't have to go to typing lessons: Just buy a book on typing, learn which finger goes to which key, and then do the exercises. Or Google to find a diagram of which fingers go on which keys. You will pick it up over a few days. I remember sitting in front of the TV and doing it during the holidays. Then you effectively spend the rest of your life practising each time you type out a document. Soon you will be able to type more quickly than you can write.

Practical ways in which typing is extremely useful:

- **Taking notes from books or articles:** If you can "touch type" then you can be reading from the book or article, and typing your notes up at the same time. This is an extremely effective way of taking notes (from a document that you have already read – see Chapter 4).
- **Taking notes during lectures:** Bring your laptop into lectures and just take your notes down there and then. A bit of tidying up afterwards will give you an amazing set of notes in next to no time.
- **Taking notes during class:** See if you can bring your laptop into school and even use it in class. "Cut and paste" any new points into

your main "framework" notes on that particular topic, so that all your notes are in the same place.

Computer safety

- **Theft:** Some people steal things – it's a shame to have to learn this lesson the hard way.
- **Damage:** Laptops are more easily damaged than you might think. Make sure you have a proper padded computer bag.
- **Insurance:** It's possible to buy insurance against theft and damage.
- **Battery use:** Laptop batteries wear out the more times you charge them. If you use it and charge it too much, a battery that starts by lasting two and a half hours might end up lasting just half an hour. If you mainly use your laptop when plugged into the mains, then take the battery out so that the battery is not constantly charging itself, and so wearing itself out.
- **Power leads:** If you are transporting a laptop around make sure that you take the power lead out before putting it in a bag, because the power connection can very easily get badly damaged.

Use the right tools: Other useful bits and pieces

- **Dictaphones are great for taking notes** from books or articles. Just dictate your notes into the Dictaphone, and then type them up afterwards. Dictate the notes sentence by sentence so that you can easily move from one to the next when you are typing it up, without having to keep looking from the book to your computer screen, and then back to the book again. You can pick up a Dictaphone very inexpensively (£30 or $50), and some mobile phones have recording functions as well.

   Bring your Dictaphone into lectures or into any class that you think would be particularly valuable to be able to listen to again. Many teachers and lecturers would prefer you ask their permission before doing this.

- **Obviously, you need a desk:** Decent size, well-lit, quiet environment. Have a big jar of pens so that you don't have to keep looking for one.

  Don't work in bed! How are you going to get to sleep if you are in the very place that you spend a lot of your time working?

  Don't work outdoors! Papers + wind + distraction = no real work being done, guaranteed!

- **Stationery:** Buy loads at the beginning of term so that you don't have to waste time constantly running to the shop. So, buy file pads in blocks of five rather than one at a time. They won't go to waste.

- **Calendar:** Pin a calendar to your wall so that you have a good visual aid to count you down to your exams and coursework hand-in dates.

- **To-do list:** Having to remember things uses up energy and causes stress. So create a "to-do list" on paper, on your computer, or even on your phone.

- **Filing your notes:** Doing this as you go along will save you time and frustration. It's tempting to let it slide, but this is such a bad idea. The stress isn't worth it! (And believe me, I have found this out from personal experience). Use a different file for each subject, and do a little bit of filing each day so that it never gets out of hand.

Have some serious fun

The most important thing is to try to be organised so that you can get lots of sleep, eat properly, allow yourself treats and spend time having fun with your friends and family. Helena

Have serious fun when you're not working: If you are doing five hours of solid and high quality work in the day, there is still quite a bit of time to get out and about. My advice is to fill these remaining hours with as much fun and enjoyment as possible. Head out with your friends and make the most of it. Seriously enjoying yourself is - or should be – an absolutely key part of your work strategy. Taking quality time off means that you come back to the books you will be relaxed, fresh, and ready to put yourself in the position to put in a very good performance when the exams come round.

See Chapter 9 for more on this indispensable component of doing well.

Essential points:

- ✓ Don't waste work! 100% of the work you do has to be useful for the exam
- ✓ If work is worth doing then make it high quality and do it with the exam in mind
- ✓ If work isn't directly useful for the exam then avoid it if possible, or else just do enough to get by
- ✓ Using a computer will save you loads of time
- ✓ To use a computer you need to know how to type
- ✓ Working efficiently will mean that you can get the grades while actually having a life

3

Organising your success

What's this chapter about?

If you think about it, all we have is time. It's the people who make best use of that time who will end up getting the best grades.

If you want good grades then quite a lot of work is going to have to be done. So when and where are you actually going to do it?

This question is particularly important at university where you are left to your own devices much more than you are at school.

The key sections here will be as follows:

- *Organising your day*
- *Beating procrastination*
- *Fitting in as much work as possible during the day*

There's quite a lot in this chapter. My advice is to read it quite quickly so you don't get bogged down.

Getting organised - The power of the list

We all know how hard it can be to really settle down and to do some solid work. The sorts of problems that we've all experienced are:

- being interrupted
- getting distracted
- worrying about whether we'll get work done
- trying to remember what things we need to do
- not knowing what to do next
- feeling overwhelmed
- feeling guilty
- feeling stressed

The human brain simply doesn't remember its own "to do" lists very well, and all this worry wastes a huge amount of energy. You can't hide from that nagging feeling that you ought to be doing something. Having to remember all these things causes a great deal of low-level stress, which wastes a ton of energy.

What do the experts say? There are a lot of good books written on "time management", and the one thing that they all have in common is that **they are all very keen on lists** (which really is the key idea here). Here's my shorter version of some of their most useful ideas:

- **Take a few minutes to actually plan your day:** Most people don't!
- **Each day create two lists** that you can consult and add to at any time. These lists are your **"Today"** list and your **"Later"** list.
- **First thing in the morning:** Create your "Today" list. Decide which things you need to do are the most important, mark these, and do them first.
- **Make use of the list during your day:** Lists are worthless unless you actually make use of them. Strike tasks off as you complete them. Keep having a quick look at your list during the day to see what you need to do. If something comes up that you don't need to do today, then add it to your "Later" list.
- **The last thing of your working day** should be to review your "Today" list and to start to compile tomorrow's "Today" list. If something has to be done on or before a specific date then quickly copy it from your "Later" list onto your calendar. Doing this will mean that you don't need to remember what you need to do the next day, and so you can relax properly.
- **Use a wall calendar** to get an overview and to help you to anticipate each term's events. Find out when the exam dates are going to be as early as you can in the course. Include social events in your calendar so that you can adjust your planning accordingly. Take the time to review your calendar at the beginning of term so that you can see if there are any "crunch" times you need to be careful of. Watch out for clashes between exams and coursework – you may need to start working earlier because of this. Have a quick look at your calendar when you are writing your lists at the beginning and the end of the day.
- **Learn roughly how long things take:** You will only be able to plan your day if you have some sort of idea of roughly how long particular tasks

are likely to take. Leave room for flexibility. The best way to estimate is to break larger tasks down into their component parts. So, rather than just writing "do essay", instead you might write:

   o *take final notes from chapter (45 minutes)*
   o *read through notes taken and think about them (30 minutes)*
   o *planning (30 minutes)*
   o *doing the actual writing (2 hours – one hour each session)*

- **When "Later" becomes "Today":** Keep half an eye on your "Later" list, and when you judge the time is right have an "Admin" morning to get this stuff off your back. Actively choose to make "Later" happen. This is especially important when you are a student, because there will always be more work that you *could* do on your academic subjects.

- **Only do one thing at a time – don't act on things immediately unless it is genuinely necessary to do so:** If something comes up, rather than doing something immediately, just write it down and deal with it later. This allows you to get on with the task that you had actually been focussing on, rather than just being dragged from one interruption to another.

- **Do you need to do it absolutely right now??** It's very rare to genuinely need to do something *absolutely immediately*. Your focus is the most precious thing you have when it comes to doing well at exams, so add whatever it was that interrupted you to your list and deal with it later. When you're studying, if you're not focussing on ONE thing, you're focussing on NOTHING. Multi-tasking doesn't really work in this part of our lives.

- **Do similar tasks in batches:** Answer all your emails, make all your phone calls and send all your texts as one activity later in the day. This as it means your focus isn't being interrupted the whole time.

- **This is the "Two Touch" approach:** I like to think of the system outlined above as "Two Touch" time management - FIRST you decide WHEN you are going to do it, THEN you DO IT.

- **Take stock regularly once a week:** Five minutes on Saturday morning might take care of this, but it's essential to ensure that nothing slips through the net.

- **This approach has to be TOTAL: Use your lists for everything (all work and all leisure).** You can only stop worrying about "what you need to do" if you have a system that you can rely on 100%. But you can only rely on a system 100% if you use it for 100% of things that you are doing. It's not about willpower, it's about having the right system in place so that you can actually stay focussed on what you are doing. Productive days don't happen by accident.

Getting organised: Other key time management tips

Know what you want to achieve: The clearer you are about your goals, the more likely you are to achieve them. Bear in mind that if you are committed to achieving one thing, you may have to sacrifice others, otherwise it's just wishful thinking.

Decide what grades you want at the beginning of the course, and then do the work required to get them. If you only decide two months before Finals that you really want a First, you've probably missed the boat. Stephen

Learn to say no to people who are likely to distract you. You are likely to keep in close contact with only a relatively small number of your school or university friends, so don't throw your results away for the sake of pleasing people who you won't be seeing much of again in a few years' time (p 56).

Where does your time go to? Do you watch too much TV? Do you check your email or your phone fifty times a day? Are you always being interrupted by texts coming in? Are you always checking Facebook? Modern technology has provided many amazing ways of working more effectively, but we all know that it also provides amazingly effective ways of wasting time.

Know when to quit: There is no point continuing to work if you are not achieving anything. (See discussion of "The art of finishing for the day" on p 150)

Don't run late: Running late is actually a huge waste of time, because if you're worrying about whether you'll be on time, this means that you can't make use of the travel time to relax a bit.

Remember stuff by leaving it at the door so that you can't walk past without noticing it.

Establish good routines: Humans are creatures of habit, so turn this to your advantage by getting into good routines for doing work. Other people will find it difficult to compete with the sheer bulk of work that you have got under your belt when it comes round to exam time.

DANGER: Obsessing about planning and doing endless "revision plans" nearer the exam can result in these getting in the way of doing much work itself.

How to beat procrastination

Momentum is key: Get the ball rolling. Once you've actually started on a piece of work it creates its own momentum - it becomes clear what you need to do, and one task will naturally follow on from another. You'll also see that doing the work on it isn't *that* bad.

It doesn't have to be perfect: In many subjects there is no ONE way that the work has to be done. Different approaches can be equally good, and will still get the top grade at the end of the day. Give yourself permission to make mistakes and to learn from them. If you are too cautious you will do next to nothing and therefore achieve next to nothing.

Practical tips for getting started:

- **Do a little bit of work on the day that you are given the assignment:** Get the ball rolling by doing a little bit of planning and thinking about the project. It's much easier to keep that ball rolling than it is to start it moving in the first place.
- **Break it into smaller chunks:** Working out specifically what you need to do will make achieving the larger task more manageable e.g. Step 1 "get relevant books from library", Step 2 "read conclusion to get overview".
- **Just do five minutes:** Set yourself the target of just spending five minutes working on that project. Anyone can manage just five minutes work! There's a good chance that you'll end up doing twenty minutes or half an hour – and you're off!
- **Just do something!** Break the ice by doing something relevant to the project. Do the very easiest or most interesting aspect of it you can think of.
- **Smaller chunks add up:** Doing half an hour a day will mean that you do close to three hours over the course of a week, creating momentum.
- **Accept that some work is really boring:** Some tasks are pretty awful, let's be honest. Referencing springs to mind. Lock yourself in your room, put on some music and just bash on with it.

- **Ambush** that task by catching it early in the day, even just as soon as you get up. Start working on it even before you have the chance to procrastinate!
- **Turn habit to your advantage:** Humans are creatures of habit, and routine is the enemy of procrastination.

Fitting in as much work as possible during the day

You are in and around school or university for a very major chunk of your week. Many people mess around in class, after class and during study periods, but in reality these are golden opportunities for getting some proper work done.

Make use of short periods of time: It's so easy to waste that forty-five minutes between classes. But work that you manage to achieve in short bursts like this makes for more free time in the evening. Don't make the mistake of thinking that you need a long and uninterrupted stretch of time ahead of you in order to do some "proper" work and really achieve something. Short work sessions are particularly useful for activities like learning and understanding, which you can't usefully do for long periods anyway.

Find somewhere you can get proper work done: Find somewhere you can work without being distracted. At university it's often an idea to head to somewhere in the library that isn't used by your classmates. Don't work with your friends – avoid them until you're taking a well-earned break. Sneaking in quick bursts of work during the day will mean that you have more time to see your friends properly later.

My advice is that you should do either do one thing or the other:

- **EITHER PLAY HARD:** When you are spending time with your friends, make the most of it.
- **OR WORK HARD:** When you are working, give it 100%. This is the flip side. "Go big or go home".

- **AVOID the halfway house** where you are *kind* of working, *kind* of talking with your friends. If you're not focussed on one activity or the other, you're getting the worst of both worlds. Either do one thing or the other.

WHY do as much work as possible during the school day? If you want great results you are going to have to do fairly significant amounts of work anyway. You may as well get as much of it done as possible during the school day, in order that that you can have as much quality free time as possible outside school. Free time during which you arrange to meet up with your friends properly is simply a lot more fun than sitting talking crap in the study area.

Preparing for class actually saves you time

> If there is designated reading before class, do it. You'll remember far more if you hear the tutor talking about what you just read, than if you do your reading after class and try to remember what the tutor said. Kirk

I personally have sat through many classes without really having a clue about what was going on. We've all been there, and we all know that the result is just boredom interrupted by occasional embarrassment.

Participation, processing and understanding: Preparing properly means that you can use your time during class to actually achieve something, rather than its just being wasted. Preparation means that you can participate in class. Crucially, participation requires your active processing of the material at hand. Active processing will produce understanding (p 163). Understanding produces good grades.

Making the most of your tutor: Think of your tutor as a valuable source of potential understanding, standing at the front of the classroom. Making the most of this resource is a smart use of your time.

When other people in your class ask questions:

- Think about how you would have answered that question
- Pay attention to the tutor's response. Even if the question isn't that good, the tutor's response may contain some nuggets of understanding that you can make use of. Jot these down and add them to your notes later. Make sure that you distinguish between things that your tutor has said and things that other students in the class have said – if the analysis belongs to another student then you can't simply rely on it.

In technical subjects like Maths and the sciences make sure you take good notes on the solutions of problems, as being able to work through as many problems as possible will be key to your revision for these topics. Don't just write down the workings – take the time to write down the reasoning for each step in the process.

Talk to your tutor at the end of class to iron out any questions that you have – either from that class or from other work you have done on the subject. One-on-one input can make all the difference, but yet most people won't be getting it.

Use classes to save you time: Preparation and participation convert wasted time into time that is really productive in terms of achieving understanding for the exam. You're going to be there anyway, and if you want good grades the work's going to have to be done at some point, so you might as well make the very most of the time you spend in class.

What's the alternative? Kicking back in class is not really *that* much fun. It's simply better use of your time to work in class and then to do something that you enjoy after the school day, when you have a much more interesting "menu" of fun stuff to choose from.

After class: The five minute review

Question: If you have just had a class on something, and still have some work to do on it to understand the work and to get your notes together, when's the best time to do that work?

Answer: As soon after that class as possible. The material will be fresh in your mind. You may remember some things that you didn't have time to write down at the time. This can be tough to motivate yourself to do, but you can gain a lot by striking while the iron is hot.

Use a computer: Taking your notes on a computer will allow you to tidy up your class and lecture notes really very quickly. Then have a think about them and add your own thoughts and ideas in square brackets. Bingo – you can have a useful set of notes, which you actually understand, extremely quickly indeed. That's smart use of time.

Don't fall behind!

> If you don't understand something – ask a question. At A level Maths I asked more questions than the rest of the class put together! I worried that I was stupider than everybody else, but I think I just wanted to understand what was going on, and wasn't embarrassed to admit that I hadn't understood something. My class was mostly boys and I think they felt it wasn't macho to admit you didn't follow something, or indeed that you cared. Helena

Not understanding something is ok. You are at school to learn – that is the whole point. Looking dumb before the exam is a lot smarter than finding out you've been dumb afterwards.

The social side of school and university

Who are you hanging around with? If you're at school and you hang around with people who are messing around the whole time, then you are much less likely to get good results. But the truth is that, after you go off to university, you will probably only keep in regular touch with 5-10 school friends. Similarly, a few years after university you will probably only be in touch with a relatively small number of friends from your student days. It's not worth sacrificing your grades for the sake of people who you will not be in touch with a mere two or three years down the road.

Who are you sitting beside? The same point applies here. If you are sitting beside someone who is keeping you back, then you will need to work harder in the evenings to compensate. But if you are sitting beside someone who is applying themselves, then this can be a big bonus, as you can help each other out.

Where are you sitting in class? Are you hiding at the back, or are you sitting somewhere where you can hear properly and chip in if you have something to contribute?

> *In classrooms, sit in the second or third row, far enough back to see the entire blackboard or PowerPoint® screen, but close enough that you can get the tutor's attention if you have a question and close enough that you can't doze off without him noticing. Kirk*

Is your whole class going to do badly? In some classes there is so much mucking around that the results of the whole class will suffer. If the class is a complete disaster it may be worth having a word with your parents or your school's head of that subject.

Avoid pointless discussions about how much work or how little work you or other people are doing. Some people brag about doing nothing but then mysteriously turn up rather well-prepared for the exams. Others brag about how much they are doing but then their results are surprisingly poor.

Extra-curricular activities: Balance is key. Playing sports, appearing in school plays can be excellent ways of relaxing. But if you want to get great results then don't let extra-curricular stuff get in the way of work, especially in crunch years when you have important exams or coursework to hand in.

> In my final year I played rugby for the university, and the training was taking up a lot of time. But I was still determined do well in the exams at the end of the year, and so I had to fit in a lot of work as well. The adjustment I made that year was simply not to socialise at all. I thought about the different parts of my life: (1) Work, (2) Sport, (3) Socialising. I knew that I couldn't manage to do all three, and so had to pick which ones I wanted to do. Playing rugby for the university was a big deal for me. Doing well at exams was something that I had worked towards for years. So my social life simply had to go. I've made up for it since though! Johnny

Teachers and lecturers: Make sure that you get on reasonably well with them, so that you can get their attention both in class and after class. Simple politeness goes a long way, and if you find their class interesting, let them know. Tutors are human beings and will like a bit of positive feedback as much as anyone else.

Lecturers: At university your lecturers and tutors are also your examiners. Anyone who has been to university will know how awkward some tutorials can be if no-one is contributing. Your tutor will appreciate your making the effort to actually say something. Although university work is marked anonymously, your tutor will often have a very good idea who has written a particular piece of work. If they like you, they will be inclined to give you better marks.

Cooperating with other students: Good relationships with other people who are keen to do well can be very useful. There is absolutely no harm in a degree of teamwork in getting the work done. Be generous when it comes to lending your notes out if someone else has missed a class - it will do you very little harm (as long as you make sure you get them back), but will mean that you can ask the other person a favour or two if you need it at some point in the future. If you are borrowing someone else's notes then make sure they are the sort of person who will have taken down good notes that will actually be useful.

Essential points:

- ✓ Actively use lists to organise your day, so that trying to remember things isn't stressing you out.
- ✓ Beat procrastination by using small bursts of work to create momentum.
- ✓ Fit in as much work as possible during the day at school or university, to maximise the quality free time you'll have after it.
- ✓ Make the most of your time in class by preparing, participating and reviewing immediately afterwards.

How to take notes quickly

(and what to do with them)

What's this chapter about?

If you can read and take notes effectively this is a massive, massive advantage – it will really get you off to a flying start.

In this chapter I am going to outline a very active approach to taking notes that will save you a lot of time.

University students in particular also need to know about which book to take notes from in the first place, about how to take useful notes from lectures, and about how to make the most of the internet.

But then what do you do with the notes once you've taken them? This chapter ends with sections on how to structure your work, and with a general overview of how to approach a topic in the first place.

Is how you take notes really that important?

Reading and taking notes is the "bread and butter" of student life. It is one of the most fundamental and basic activities that people do at school and university. Whatever you are studying, you will never really get away from reading and taking notes.

It's the foundation on which a lot of your exam preparation is based. Getting this right will mean that you are heading in the right direction from the start. It will also save you huge amounts of time.

The hippopotamus and the fighter pilot

- **The hippopotamus** wallows in his mud bath. He wallows this way, he wallows that. It's a fairly comfortable place to be, and a lot of mud gets wallowed in, but not much actually gets done.
- **The fighter pilot** has a defined mission which he carries out with maximum efficiency and speed. He's got a plan and is back at base before you know it.

How not to do it: Wallowing in the mud bath

There are two **classic mistakes** that people often make when taking notes, one mistake leading to the other:

- **Method:** Reading the chapter or article from the first page and start taking notes as you go along is a slow and painstaking process. Often you end up practically copying it out word for word, an switching between the material and your notes means that you have to constantly keep finding your place.

- **End result:** Basically you end up with far too many notes. In the exam you won't have time to write that much. Taking more notes than you will be able to make use of in the exam is a waste of effort.

My note-taking technique was and remains appalling; I'd write down far too much and then not have time to review it all. Clarke.

Taking notes selectively: The fighter pilot's approach

What do we want? We want notes that are going to be useful (for the exam or for coursework), and we want to get them as quickly as possible. You need to have the exam in mind from the very first moment that you pick up a book. In this sense your revision begins on day one.

The way to think about it is that you are trying to **"gut"** the book to get the information that you need from it. You want to get maximum benefit from this book, and to do so in as efficient a way as possible. You want to **"juice"** the book – you want to squeeze the goodness out of the sections you have chosen to read.

Making the effort to take an active approach: This kind of reading takes a lot of energy and focus. It's the opposite of lazily flipping your way through a book, or passively beginning at the very first page and reading all your way through to the end.

Here is how to do it:

Before you even pick up a book...

- *Make sure that you are reading the right book:* Reading and taking notes is a major investment of time, even if you are doing it right. (See p 73)
- *Find out something about it:* Knowing a little something about what you are looking for will make a huge difference. Your teacher or lecturer may have briefly referred to the author's argument – how did they put it? Maybe looking at Wikipedia or Googling around for 5 minutes might give you an idea as to where the book's argument is headed.

Step 1:   Work out what you are trying to get from the material

Ask yourself: "What do I need from this book?"

- *How much do I already know about this topic?* This is a great question because it makes you approach the reading in a very targeted way, with the practical goal of finding out stuff that adds to your existing knowledge. What do I need to find out?
- *What level of detail do I need here?* Do I want detailed notes or am I simply looking for one specific piece of information?
- *Read with a purpose.* Like the fighter pilot, you must have a plan. Do your reading with the end result in mind. Rather than just reading, you're reading to find out particular stuff.

Be selective: not all the contents of the book will be equally important. It all depends what you want to get from the book. Figuring out what you actually need to know for the exam is a key part of the work you need to do.

What are you looking for?

- an outline of the book's basic argument?
- a set of pretty detailed notes that can serve as your foundation notes for a particular topic, or a particular term's work?
- information about a particular topic that is mentioned in the book?

Read actively and ask questions of the material, rather than just letting it wash over you.

Step 2: Get an overview of what you are going to be able to get from this material

- Read the **chapter's title** carefully, and also any **headings within the chapter**.
- Is there a **summary** at the end of the book or at the end of each chapter? Check. It may not be called "summary". Also check the first few pages of the conclusion. Finally have a quick look in the introduction.
- Some articles contain an **abstract** or very short summary right at the beginning.
- **The conclusion: Begin reading here.**   The danger with the introduction is that the author may spend too much time "setting the scene".

  Use the conclusion to get a clear idea as to what the author has been arguing for. Use it to find out if there has been a particular question the author has been trying to answer, and their answer to it – in brief.

Knowing what the author is arguing for makes a huge difference to how you make use of the rest of the book. For one thing, you know the direction in which he or she is heading. More practically, it means that when taking notes you just need to find points that support the author's overall argument.   You don't need to follow the whole argument in painstaking detail – for to do so would involve copying out practically the entire book. Instead, select the most interesting and eye-catching points and pieces of evidence that you can find.

Targeting your note-taking in this way will make it much more selective – and so much, much quicker! You don't need to spend hour after hour taking detailed notes on every book you read. There is no point in taking more notes than you will have time to make use of in the exam.

- **How to read a chapter:** Read the first paragraph, then the last. (This is a bit like reading the conclusion and the introduction of the book as a whole). Then read any headings and the first sentence of each paragraph. This gets you a good idea of where that particular chapter is going. Survey what you're reading to get the lie of the land.
- **Use the index** if there is one particular thing that you are interested in from a book. Don't automatically go to where the thing you are interested in is first referenced – instead go to where it is referenced as being discussed in multiple pages (e.g. 55-59) as you are likely to find much more material here.

Step 3: Read and mark the text (but don't take notes as you go along!)

The first sentence of each paragraph often gives a very good idea as to the contents of the rest of that paragraph. This technique is known as "signposting" and will be used by most good authors. It is something that you can use as part of your own essay-writing technique (p 98).

Convert statements into questions: If a section that you are reading is on "Causes of migration into Europe" then turning this into a question – "What were the causes of migration into Europe?" - will help you think about the material more actively. You are now hunting for information, rather than being squashed by large quantities of text.

New words: Find out what new terminology means early on, otherwise this will slow your reading down. Dictionaries are available online.

Speed-reading books advocate reading down the middle of the page, but trying to widen your vision while doing so, so that more text is being caught in your field of vision. You're not trying to read every word here, but rather to get a sense of the points that are being made. Just skim through it.

Mark the book as you are going along:

- **Buy your own copy** if you can so you can mark the text and break the spine so it sits more easily. If it's not your own copy then use pencil and then rub it out afterwards.
- **Underlining or highlighting everything is a complete waste of time** —you might as well be underlining nothing!
- **Underline words, rather than whole sentences or paragraphs.** Marking the key words will make it quicker to take notes later on. If you are underlining everything, you might as well be underlining nothing.
- **You need a system for marking which points are most important:** I draw one line at the side of the page if the point is probably worth noting, but I draw two or even three lines for the most important points.
- **Jot down any thoughts** that occur to you in square brackets at the top or the bottom of the page. Think actively about the text rather than just passively going through it. Understanding starts right at the beginning of the process.
- **Who is the author and why is he or she writing this book?** If you are reading a textbook on "Organic Chemistry" this question is not going to be particularly relevant. However if you are reading a book with more of an argument to it, you need to know and show awareness of where the author is coming from. What are they arguing for? Whose side are they on?

Step 4: Take notes AFTER you have read the material

Read first, and then take notes: Taking notes as you are going along will massively slow you down. For one thing, you will have to keep finding your place in the text and in your notes. For another, you don't want to find yourself writing out the same point more than once, as this is a waste of time, and the same point may be expressed on multiple occasions. However, if you find the same point expressed slightly differently, and this different way of putting it will help your understanding, then write it down.

Don't take too many notes: There is little point in taking more notes that you will be able to remember for the exam. You can always come back to that book or article later.

Content of your notes:

- Use point form and bullet points. You don't have to copy out the text or even use full sentences.
- Break your notes down into main points and sub-points. This will make the material easier to use for revision, and will also force you to think about it as you are going along.
- Paraphrase the material: Putting it into your own words will kick-start the process of understanding. The whole point here is to take notes in the way that will be the most use when it comes to preparing for the exam.
- Put your own thoughts and questions in square brackets [like this]. Doing so means that you are thinking actively about the material and so starting to understand it.
- If you come across a short quotation that would be useful for the exam then put it in quotation marks.
- Use abbreviations.
- Capitalise or underline key words as you go along. This will help you when you come back to use this material when preparing for the exam.
- Back up theoretical points with concrete examples.

Advanced point: **Put the real substance of the point first, then the detail backing this up at the end.** This will help you to remember it when it comes to revision. Example:

- o *How not to take notes*: "1807 Slave Trade Act. Passed by UK Parliament. Abolished slave trade but not slave ownership"
- o *How to take notes*: "Slave trade abolished but not slave ownership. UK Parliament passed Slave Trade Act 1807".
- o *Why is the second way better?* This is a subtle point but quite an important one. The second way moves from the real substance of what happened, through the point of who did it, and finally onto the detail of exactly when it happened. Doing it this way means that your notes start with the real meat of this issue, supplemented by the details. I think that it's easier to remember points that start with the real substance of the issue, rather than notes that start with very particular and slightly abstract details such as the name and date of a particular Act of Parliament.

Make use of all available tools to help you:

- **Dictaphone:** Highlight your notes and then come back to them at the end with a dictaphone. Record them all onto your dictaphone (which will just take a few minutes). Then play the notes back on the dictaphone and type them up. Make sure that you record your notes in short chunks of about ten seconds at a time so that you can type them up easily. Ten seconds will be about the length of a sentence, and so you can play it back to yourself, remember it and then type it up directly onto your computer.
- **Voice-recognition software:** This is where you speak into your computer, usually through a headset, and then it types out automatically for you. In my experience it's pretty good but not *quite* accurate enough for regular use.
- **"Book chairs":** These hold the book open, allowing you to take notes directly onto your computer.

Referencing: Do your referencing AFTER you take your notes. It's quicker this way, because you're just concentrating on one task at a time (p 126).

Step 5: Immediately after taking your notes...

- **Review:** Have a quick read at your notes at the end to make sure that they make sense.
- **Understand:** Now is a great time to start thinking about the issues you have been taking notes on, given that the ideas are already in your head. Starting to actually understanding the material will be crucial to your performance in the exam. Use the thoughts already sloshing around inside your head to get the process of understanding off to a flying start.
- **Evaluate:** Did you answer the questions that made you want to read that book in the first place, or do you need to read something else?

Activity vs Passivity: The strategy outlined above is an **active** process in contrast to the flawed and passive approach of just starting to take notes from the first page, and working your way through to the end. You actually have to almost attack the book, and need to approach it with this kind of determined mindset. It's the mindset of the fighter pilot rather than the hippopotamus.

Organising your notes: Pick one source of information to use as a framework for each topic

This is a really, really important section. It applies especially to university students

For each topic of work that you cover, you need to know where your basic framework of notes is coming from. Your framework is the backbone of your notes, your fundamental notes on that particular subject. Your framework will contain the bulk of your notes. Once you have got your framework into place you can slot any other useful stuff you come across into it.

Where might you get your basic notes from? Pick one:

- Your textbook OR (NOT "and"!)
- Outlines provided by your tutor OR (NOT "and"!)
- Some other book that you have selected

In practical terms, the question is this: Where are you lifting your basic notes from? You can't make it all up yourself, so where are you going to get the bulk of your notes from?

When studying a particular thing it is really important that you draw your fundamental notes from one particular source – and one only. Doing so will mean that your notes are both comprehensive and coherent:

- **Comprehensive** in the sense that a good author will have included everything that you need to know – his analysis will be more than adequate for the purposes of school at any rate.
- **Coherent** in that, given that you are drawing on the work of a single author, he is not likely to contradict himself. Each aspect of what he writes is likely to fit nicely with the other points he makes.

CLASSIC MISTAKE: Piecing together your own "patchwork quilt" of fundamental notes on a particular topic will take you a very, very long time indeed, and will produce a result that is neither comprehensive or coherent. Yes, even if you have lifted most of your fundamental notes from one source you will want to add bits and pieces to it to add to your understanding. But there is no need to reinvent the wheel.

Understanding: Crucially, it is vital to actually understand the contents of your basic notes before trying to develop any more detailed views or opinions on a certain topic. If you don't understand your basic notes then you will not be in a position to add further material. You will add it in the wrong way, or the level of detail involved will just confuse you.

Adding to your fundamental notes: Only once the foundation of your work for that topic is in place should you add further details to your notes. These are supplementary - they add to and decorate the solid framework of your essential understanding of the topic.

Organising your notes: The Master Document

One way of keeping your notes in order is by creating a Master Document.

This is a large Word® (computer) document that contains absolutely all your notes on a particular topic. It can contain a term's or even a year's work on a particular topic.

Advantages to creating a Master Document:

- **You know where all your notes are** on that particular topic.
- **It saves time:** Writing material out twice - "duplication" - is a waste of time. If you know that something is already in your Master Document, then you don't need to bother writing it out again.
- **It will help you to structure your notes**, both on paper and in your head, making it easier to see how different aspects of a particular subject fit into the bigger picture. Structure is key - if you haven't got the material organised on paper, how are you going to get it straight in your head?

How to create a Master Document:

- **Create a Master Document** containing your "framework" notes (p 70) and then slot in any supplementary information and your own thoughts around these.
- **Use a computer:** You can only really create a document of this size if you are using a computer. It also means that you can use your Master Document to create summary notes for revision very quickly indeed by means of cut and paste. Don't forget to back it up!!

For revision you can break it up into smaller chunks if you find these easier to work with. Each chunk can contain all your notes on that particular topic.

To find your place in a larger document write "FROM HERE" and then use the search function (Control + F) to find these words (and your place).

Choosing the right book: A brief word on reading lists

At university, particularly in the "arts" subjects such as History or English Literature, you will usually be given a reading list at the beginning of each term.

Some are more realistic than others: Many lecturers use a "star" system to indicate which are the more important items for you to have a look at, which is useful. However in many cases it would be virtually impossible to complete the amount of reading that you are expected to do in theory.

Should I try to read everything? Very often you shouldn't. Don't make the mistake of assuming that simply reading every item on the list will get you the best grades. It won't. In fact, if you tried to read every item on the list you would probably get a very poor grade, the reason being that you would end up with FAR TOO MUCH INFORMATION, and that you would have spent all your time READING stuff rather than actually THINKING about the material you have read about. One of the themes of this book is that it's TAKING THE TIME TO ACTUALLY UNDERSTAND the material that you have encountered that will help you do well in the exam.

Why do some lecturers do this? Often that there are debates that the lecturer wants you to be aware of. Knowing that Jones' classic work written in 1953 provides the foundation for one side of the current debate, your lecturer will add Jones' 500 page book to your reading list. Knowing that Atwood's 1962 response underpins the other side, Atwood's devastating 625 page counter-attack will also be added to the list. But in reality there will be much shorter works that neatly summarise Jones' and Atwood's magnificent contributions, and which also – crucially – will evaluate them and in so doing will give you something intelligent to say. It's simply not realistic for an undergraduate to read or evaluate such huge - and hugely complicated - works.

In the sections that follow I set out my own strategy:

- Make careful use of the **internet** or even children's books to give you an overview of the topic (see p 81).
- **Pick one source of information** to use as a framework for each topic. Rather than wading through long original contributions, find a book that summarises the debates and evaluates them. Then take the time to have a good think about them yourself.
- **Find useful books that haven't been mentioned** on the reading list. There will usually be books that would be incredibly useful to know about for doing your course, but that haven't been mentioned at all by your lecturers. (see p 77)
- Get maximum benefit from **lectures** so that you are off to a flying start. (see p 78)
- Get maximum benefit from **class** as discussed earlier. (see p 53)

By all means come back to the "classic works" towards the end of the process to put the "icing on the cake". By this stage you will hopefully have a solid grasp of the debates in that topic and so have some idea what to actually look out for.

The general point here is that you need to approach reading lists both critically and selectively, and with your brain switched to "ON". Heading off to live in the library for the next six months isn't any fun, and isn't the best way of getting top results either!

Choosing the right book: Books they may not be telling you about

The most important hour's work you do should take place right at the very start of the course: If you are going to work effectively, you need to make sure that you are using the right tools.

Invest your time wisely: Reading and taking notes is very time-consuming, and so it is extremely important to make sure that you are reading and taking notes from the right book.

The point here is this: **It is extremely likely that there is a book or books out there that would be of immense use to you in your preparation for the exam, but that your teacher or lecturer has not actually mentioned to you.** It is of the absolute utmost importance that you get your hands on this book, for it will provide you with the material you need to help you do extremely well in the exam.

Let's talk more specifically about some examples of the kind of book that might be really helpful:

Example Number One: The "Lit Crit" Book

The classic example of this kind of book is the "literary criticism" or "lit crit" book in English Literature. Crit Books are basically books of notes on particular works of literature. So, if you are studying "The Great Gatsby" there will be a number of "crit" books on market, which act as companions to this and to other actual works of literature. They will contain discussion of the characters of the book, the themes, the imagery – basically most of what you need to know for the exam.

When I studied English for A Level there came a point when I realised that my teacher was not going to get me my "A" and that I was therefore going to have to do a lot of the work myself. In this situation "Crit Books" really helped me by discussing the themes and characters in the books that we were studying. Needless to say, their existence had not been mentioned at all in class. Soraya

Example Number Two: Revision Guides

"Revision guides" give an outline and an overview of the material in any particular course. There are big pluses and big minuses with this type of book:

- **PLUS:** Revision guides can often contain extremely useful material. They are often written by teachers and examiners who know exactly what the exam will require. They will explain the material slightly differently to the way your tutor did which can really help you to understand it.
- **MINUS:** Given that they are written with a view to benefitting students over the complete range of ability, they may be too simple, and so taking them as the "last word" on any given subject would be a mistake.

"Companion books" are quite similar to revision guides: They don't so much cover the same ground as textbooks, but rather aim to give some context to and illuminate the more central works in some way. An example of these would be the anatomy colouring in books (where learn by colouring in in the different parts of the human body) – they help you understand the main textbooks by offering some kind of different content.

Example Number Three: Books that give an overview of the debate

> When I was preparing for my dissertation I was given the usual reading list of books and articles. But the most useful thing I read wasn't actually on that list at all. Searching around on Amazon I came across an amazing book that summarised all the recent debates on this topic. It got fantastic reviews and was published only a few years ago, so it was really up to date. Matt

Use the internet to find out if there is one book out there that might save you reading five others. Spend some time hunting around on Amazon and Google. Do not assume that the most useful book will be on the reading list.

Example Number Four: Short books by high-quality authors

Your tutor will often base their teaching on a particular textbook, and get you to take notes from this.

In addition, there are a number of reasons that it might be useful to have a further book to refer to:

- **Brevity:** It might be shorter, for the reason that it expresses what you need to know more concisely.
- **Perspective:** It might express ideas in a slightly different way, one that you understand more easily.

Here is the kind of book you are looking for:

Size: You want a slim volume, rather than a massive book. Slim volumes will tell you all that you need to know for the purposes of school. Massive books will be too detailed; there is no point in wading through a pile of detail that you don't actually need to know. Simplicity is key.

Author: Books usually contain some information on the author. Alternatively use Google to find out who they are, by Googling their name along with their subject area. (Example: Claire Marshall, English Literature). You want an author who is either an examiner or who is teaching at a university.

Level: Ideally the book will be just slightly more difficult than you actually need. It is much easier to summarise and simplify the ideas of a single slightly more difficult book, rather than trying to piece together a patchwork quilt of ideas lifted from lots of easier books. See more on this point in the next section (p 69).

When it was written: Preferably recently, so that the author will be able to refer to the most recent contributions to the subject that you are studying.

Example Number Five: Did they write an article?

Authors will often have written an article or a chapter with more or less the same content as their book. The trick is finding it. There are a variety of ways of doing this:

- **Google their name to find their profile** at the university they teach it. These often contain complete lists of their publications. See if there is an article that looks as if it covers the same ground as their book.
- **Look at bibliographies in other books.** Bibliographies are where an author lists all the books and other material that he or she has drawn on to write his own work. They are usually located at the back. Keep an eye on references in the footnotes as well.
- **Ask** your lecturer.

When to do this: Get your hands on a copy of this kind of book early on in the course, so that you can get the maximum benefit from it.

How to find the books that they are not telling you about:

- **Ask your tutor** if there is "anything else they would recommend".
- **Ask a friend** in the year above or in your own year.
- **Search through Amazon** on the internet: Put "the Great Gatsby" into Amazon, and you will come across a lot of stuff that could come in very useful indeed (e.g. "Crit Books"). Read the reviews by other people who have bought the book to get some idea of the contents and how useful it might be. You can often get some idea about what's contained in the book by using Amazon's "look inside" function or by seeing if the book is on "Google books".
- **Libraries - you need to know how to use them properly:** Universities usually have sessions at the beginning of the year to teach this. Boring, but essential. If you are in second year and find that you don't know how to use the library, see if you can tag along with the first years to get up to speed.
- **Hunting around in the library:** If you are getting books from the library make sure you have a good look at the other books in that section. There may be some useful books there that your tutor hasn't mentioned. Do this at the beginning of term so that you can get maximum benefit. Go even before term begins so that you can get your hands on the most useful books.
- **Books or articles that your tutor has written him or herself** are the best way of finding out what they really think, what they are really interested in, and the style that they prefer to see. But some tutors are very reluctant to recommend books that they themselves have written. If your tutor has have a personal profile page on the university website it may well list all their publications.

Taking notes in lectures

Finding out what they want: At university the lecturers are your examiners, so it's worth paying very close attention to what they're saying!

Attendance: Decide what you are going to do at the very beginning of the course. Use the first lecture to find out if they are going to be useful. There is rarely much point in attending only some of the lectures in a series, as the material often runs over from one lecture to another.

Go over the notes of the previous lecture before the next: You will understand a lot more and so take better notes if you have some idea of what the topic is in advance. Thinking about what you already know about this topic will help you tune in and also to appreciate that this could be a good learning opportunity.

Decide what you want to get out of the lecture: Perhaps you know nothing about the topic, in which case you can try to get down pretty much everything the lecturer says, to get you off to a flying start. On the other hand, if you have already done a lot of work on that topic, then you might just need to note down a few finishing touches, or suggestions for further reading that you haven't come across yet.

General tactic = Write down everything your lecturer says: If you don't get everything, then borrow someone's notes afterwards to supplement your own.

Make use of handouts and online materials: These may mean that you don't need to get down every word during the lecture itself. If you are using a computer you might be able to cut and paste them into your own notes.

Use technology: If you have a laptop and know how to type, it is possible to get down pretty much every word. Arrive early to give yourself time to get set up. Tidy up the inevitable typing mistakes later on, and you have a useful set of notes. Use a dictaphone – record your lecture and supplement your notes from this later.

Use abbreviations rather than whole sentences. So for example:

- ∴ - means "therefore". But if you write this symbol upside down it means "because".
- ≈ - means "approximately the same as"
- ≠ - means "not the same as"
- → - means "in consequence"
- cf - means "compare with" or "consult"

- Make up your own symbols – there are no rules here. e.g. I use a P with two little lines sprouting out of it to mean "in parallel with".
- If there is a word that you are going to have to write constantly e.g. "Roman Empire" then just abbreviate it to RE.

Put your own thoughts in square brackets: [Listen actively by noting down any questions or "understanding" points that occur to you]

Use your margins: Use the space in the margin to indicate the broader theme of the lecture, and to signpost the contents written in the main part of the page. American students often expand the margin at the left hand side of the page by ruling a line down the page about a quarter of the way across, giving them a bit more space to indicate the contents, and to add their personal notes. Put question marks in the margin if you miss a point and leave a gap so that it's quicker to fill in later on.

Listen particularly to find out about:

- **Current academic debates in that particular subject:** There are areas of dispute and uncertainty at the frontiers of every subject. Your lecturer will know all about these, but as a student it is often difficult to get a grasp of where these areas lie. Writing down your lecturer's summaries and descriptions of different people's perspectives can often save you the need to read the books or articles that they have written.

- **Contents of books on the reading list:** Lecturers often summarise the contents of key works on the reading list in a few sentences. Make sure you get these down, because it will be a lot quicker and easier to approach longer works if you know exactly what you are looking for. If you know what the key point is, then you will just need a few details to decorate that key point and to back it up. Paying close attention in the lecture may mean that you hardly need to read some of the items on the reading list.

Further reading: Use the lecture to help you decide what's important on the reading list, and follow up on any suggestions about further reading. Many people will have attended the lecture, but few students will bother to look at this extra material. Taking some brief notes from it will allow you to stand out from the crowd.

Pay particular attention to the first and last things that the lecturer says: Sometimes these points can seem almost casual, but often they are extremely important in giving a context and structure to the content of the lecture, and in indicating how the lecturer (your examiner) views the topic overall. Make sure you write them down.

Key points are often indicated by pauses to allow everyone to write that particular thing down. Put a star beside anything that the lecturer takes the time to emphasise or to repeat.

Have a word with the lecturer at the end: If you have any questions this is a great time to get some valuable one on one input from the lecturer. Most people waste this opportunity.

Review immediately afterwards: Tidy up your notes straight after the lecture. You may remember some points that you had forgotten. But more importantly this is a good time to start to think about the topic, given that the material is fresh in your head. What were the big ideas? Was there a question that the lecturer was trying to ask?

The concrete and the theoretical: You need both, and using one can help you to understand the other - if the lecturer gives a concrete example, ask yourself "What is the theoretical point here?", but, on the other hand, if the lecturer puts forward a principle ask yourself "Is there a good example to back this up?"

Your lecture notes and your other notes: How are you going to use these lecture notes? Are they going to be the backbone of your notes on this topic? Or are you going to use them to supplement notes that you have got from another source by means of slotting them into your main "framework" notes on that topic? (See p 69)

In the exam be careful of just regurgitating the lecture notes back to the examiner. Many other people will be doing this, and so it's not going to make you stand out from the crowd.

Shouldn't I be more selective? Some other books suggest that you should just write down "themes" or "key points" in lectures. But the problem with this "selective approach" is that you simply may not know what to select, especially if the lecture is introducing you to that particular subject. Given that it is very possible to get down pretty much everything your lecturer says, why not just try to get it all down, and then work out how you're going to use it once you know a bit more about what's going on?

Finding material on the internet

In a nutshell: There is some good stuff on the internet and it can give you a really good overview of a topic, especially in the early stages. But you have to be extremely careful.

> When I was just starting a module on the Roman Emperor Tiberius I did a bit of Googling and came across some documents written by an academic at the University of Pennsylvania, basically summarising Tiberius' reign and the key points about him. It gave me a brilliant head start for that whole term's work. Matt

Accuracy: A lot of material available on the internet is simply inaccurate. Many people posting on the internet have some kind of political agenda, or are just lunatics. However if you find something on a university's website it is probably going to be ok.

Wikipedia: Can be useful to get an overview of a subject at the beginning of term. However, given that anyone can contribute to it and change the content of the articles, you shouldn't rely on its complete accuracy. Many university lecturers don't like Wikipedia so don't mention that you used it.

Your university's library will probably have subscribed to **journals** that you can access online through their website. Journal articles may also be available through the archive "**JSTOR**" which your university almost certainly subscribes to.

Overview: How to approach a topic

So often doing well in a particular topic boils down to becoming very familiar indeed with the contents of the right book. You have to carefully pick the right book, take good notes on the contents, and then – crucially – spend enough time actually understanding what the author is saying. If you have picked a good author then he or she will have included most of what you need to know on that topic

The real work is trying to understand it: The hard part is taking the time to actually think about and understand what the author is saying. Most people forget about this, or conveniently forget about it because it takes quite a lot of effort.

What we're aiming for: The outcome of this process is that you will have really understood the analysis of someone who really knows what they are talking about. This means that you, in turn, will really know what you are talking about. You will therefore be in the position to actually answer the questions that come up in the exams.

Giving them what they want: In the words of a friend of mine who did very well indeed at Oxford, "It's all about singing from the right hymn sheet". So, find the right hymn sheet, become very familiar indeed with its contents.

What you need to do is this:

1. Carefully choose which source you're going to take your notes from, whether that's your tutor's notes, a textbook, etc.
2. Take the notes efficiently.
3. Take your time to understand them properly.
4. Supplement your basic notes with some other material and your own thoughts.
5. Understand your notes as a whole.

You will then be in the position to:

1. Summarise your notes.
2. Understand them further.
3. Learn the material.
4. Practise using the material.

5. *Then, crucially, you will be in the position to* **APPLY** *what you have understood in the exam*

There is no neat separation between "work" and "revision": The work that you are doing needs to be geared towards the exam from day one. You need to be actively trying to understand the material right from the very beginning of the course. Understanding the material will allow you to remember it in the exam and to apply it to the questions that the examiner actually asks.

Essential points:

✓ When taking notes actively "juice" the text by scanning conclusions, headings and the first line of each paragraph. Take notes after reading, rather than when you are going along.

✓ Find the extremely useful book that you have not been told about!

✓ In lectures try to get down every word and review afterwards.

✓ The internet is an amazing resource, but contains a lot of crap as well.

✓ Get your fundamental notes on each topic from one source, rather than trying to create a "patchwork quilt" from scratch.

✓ Creating one large document with all your notes on that subject "The Master Document"

✓ Understand your basic notes as you are going along before you start to add to them significantly.

5

Perfect essays made easy

What's this chapter about?

In many different subjects, the ability to write a good essay will take you a very long way. This chapter tells you how to do it.

We'll look at the following issues:

➢ What is an essay actually testing?
➢ The importance of answering the question
➢ How do I "answer the question"?
➢ Introductions
➢ The body of the essay
➢ Conclusions
➢ Essays at school
➢ Advanced essay-writing technique
➢ How to write well

How to write an essay: What is an essay actually testing?

What is the examiner actually looking for? Why have they asked you to write an essay in the first place?

An essay is testing:

1. Your **knowledge** of the subject
2. Your **ability to apply your knowledge to the question set**

Most people know about point (1) but forget about point (2). Many people don't seem to realise that writing an essay is not just about *what you know*, it's about applying *what you know* to *actually answering the question the examiner has asked*.

How to write an essay: The importance of answering the question

The point coming up is really, really important. Grasping this and starting to put it into practice has the potential to significantly affect your grades:

** You absolutely must attempt to directly answer the question that the examiner has actually set **

WARNING, WARNING!! This sounds so simple, and yet so many people get it completely wrong:

CLASSIC MISTAKE NUMBER 1 is that of spotting a word that you recognise and then simply writing all you know about that particular topic. The danger is that on seeing the magic word "Baldwin" or "George VI" you simply vomit out everything you know about them.

> *Don't just start writing vaguely on that particular topic.   You have to answer the question. Sounds obvious but most people are too afraid of giving a "wrong answer" so just waffle on.   Kelly*

> *I've always thought the most important thing in writing an essay was the ability consistently through the essay to actually answer the question set i.e. relevance. An obvious point perhaps but I find it is not always easy to achieve. Jeremy.*

Just writing everything you know about that topic is SO OBVIOUS to the examiner, who will have seen this mistake a thousand times before. Tragically, you kind of know some stuff, but have not taken the time to THINK and so to actually apply it to the question in front of you.

YES, this approach demonstrates some relevant general knowledge of the topic. YES, what you end up writing may be somewhat relevant to the question that has been asked. BUT If you just vomit out everything you know on that topic, the examiner can only give you a mediocre mark.

CLASSIC MISTAKE NUMBER 2 is that of writing out the essay that you have planned on that particular topic, rather than actually answering the question the examiner has asked.

> *Don't just start writing out the essay you have planned - the essay that you would like to have been asked about. This, of course, seems obvious. But clearly it isn't, because loads of people completely mess up exams by taking the ball and running, without stopping to consider what direction they should be running in. Owe*

> *Answer the question set, not the question you wish it was. Liz*

> *Most important is to answer the question (and not deliver some pre-prepared answer) Kelly*

The **classic mistake** here is that of writing out YOUR essay, whereas what the examiner wants is to see HIS or HER question answered.

You will have to adapt what you know: Even slight differences in wording to the question that you have planned for may require a very significantly different answer. The whole emphasis of your argument may have to change. The whole point is that you have to adapt what you know to what has actually been asked.

DANGER: As soon as you find yourself thinking "SNAP! Great this is pretty much the same as the answer to the somewhat similar question that I revised for – I'll just write that out!" STOP and THINK. It's not the same question. It's a different question. Resist the temptation to start writing. Writing is tempting because you feel that you are doing something. But what you are doing is heading for a mediocre mark. Be strong: avoid just starting to answer the question you wish it was. Answer the question in front of you, not the one that you have prepared!!

The crucial ingredient: Understanding

You will only be able to directly answer the examiner's question if you genuinely understand the subject-matter that you are going to be writing about. Knowing quite a bit about the subject is a good start, but it isn't enough.   In order to apply your knowledge, you actually need to understand it properly. For this reason Chapter 10 on "Understanding" is the most important chapter in this book.

You need to adapt what you know to the question at hand. This requires thought – you will need to take some time in the exam to think about how to do this. For this reason the time you spend planning your answers is the most important part of any exam. See Chapter 13 on Exam Technique.

How to answer the question (1): Pay very, very close attention indeed to the particular words and language used

The examiner has chosen the wording of the question for a particular reason, and will have chosen the precise words used very carefully and deliberately. You will need to discuss these explicitly in your answer.

In practice: Underline the key words and think about them. Writing the question out again in the exam is an option. On one level this is a waste of time. But it can really make you pay attention to the exact wording used by the examiner.

Every word has particular meaning and implications. You need to put them under the microscope:

- o   Say what they mean.
- o   Say what they imply: each word in the dictionary contains certain hints and resonances.
- o   Say why that choice of word is interesting or important.

Discuss the words used "out loud" in your essay. Your whole answer needs to flow from your understanding of the precise meaning and suggestion of the particular words used in the question.

*The most practical tip I can give is READ THE
QUESTION. Read it properly. Re-read it. Don't
even think of putting pen to paper before
you've really understood what the question is
asking of you. And then read it again to make
sure! I found it useful to underline the most
pertinent words within the question. I would
also never start properly writing for five
minutes, which I would spend digesting my task
and possibly scribbling some personal notes as
to how I would structure my response. I am not
the smartest person in the world; nor have I
revised thoroughly enough for any exam I've
ever sat (as far as I recall); but I was
always quite good at sitting exams themselves,
and I think this is probably what saved me.
Owe*

How to answer the question (2): Attack the question

Criticise the question's assumptions: The question will make certain
assumptions. Work out what they are, state what they are, and then
question whether or not they are correct. You need to note that the
question assumes x or y, and then go on to say that this is not necessarily
the case. See p 89 for a detailed example of how this is done.

Do not accept the question at face value: A docile, uncritical approach
will set you straight on course for a mediocre mark. So, question the
question. Analyse it. Argue with it.

Get into an argument: Examiners love it when you argue with them.
They like a good fight, so give them one. The point here is that you will
get a lot of extra credit for applying your knowledge to the question at
hand. The fact that you are arguing with the question shows precisely
that you are applying your knowledge to it.

*The best essay mark I ever got was when I
quoted directly from a book by the examiner*

and said her view was 'patently nonsense'.
Should've done it more often. Clarke

Prove your case with evidence: You can only argue with the examiner if you have evidence to back up your view. Make sure that you include evidence of this kind in your revision notes so that you can produce it in the exam. Choose pieces of evidence that are particularly striking or interesting. You should also be constantly on the lookout for good quotations that you can make use of. Short ones are best!

When to attack the question: Some people make the mistake of thinking that you should set out the arguments in the body of the essay, but then only properly engage with and answer the question in the conclusion. This is incorrect. Your whole essay should be an attack on the question, and as such an attempt to answer it directly. Each paragraph needs to be directed towards answering the question that has actually been asked, starting with the introduction. (See p 101 for more advanced points on this issue).

How to write an essay: Answering the question – looking at a concrete example

Let's put what we are talking about into practice by picking apart a typical question. Here's a question from a history exam that I found on the internet.

"To what extent was Baldwin responsible for Conservative success?"

I have deliberately chosen a topic that I know next to nothing about, so that we can focus on the *technique* of attacking the question, rather than on the *particular content* of the answer.

Notice that my focus will be on:

- Looking very carefully at the words actually used
- Attacking the question by questioning the question itself.

"To what extent was Baldwin responsible for Conservative success?":

- **What's the *key word* in this question?** The key word in this question is *extent*. We have to look at the extent to which Baldwin was responsible for Conservative success, but then to set this in the context of other factors that contributed towards their success. Try to spot the key word in the question.
- **What *assumptions* does the question make?** The question assumes that the Conservatives were successful. Were they successful? How successful were they? Were they more successful at some times / in some places / with some voters than others?
- **Answering the question: Baldwin.** What was his relationship to Conservative success? What did he do that might have promoted success?   Did he do anything else that actually undermined Conservative success? Did he in fact do very much at all? How did people at that time think he affected Conservative success?
- **Answering the question:** Other reasons for Conservative success. The key word "extent" implies that there were factors other than Baldwin that affected Conservative success. Our answer needs to flow from the wording of the question, and so we need to consider these other factors. What were they? Were there other reasons within the Conservative Party (e.g. other personalities, institutional developments)? Were there other reasons outside the Conservative Party (e.g. general economic factors, weakness of the opposition)?

Why attacking the question is such a beautiful thing: You'll notice that despite the fact I know next to nothing about Baldwin, I have still been able to say quite a lot in response to the question posed. The examiner loves to see students who directly engage with the question by analysing and questioning the precise words that he or she has chosen to use. *But* *the real beauty of attacking the question is that it actually gives you quite a lot to say even if you don't actually know that much about the topic.*

> If you know what you're doing, you actually don't need to have a lot of factual knowledge in order to answer a question well. Frankie

But it's not the end of the story: "Attacking the question" is the sort of "analytical" approach that is precisely what the examiner is looking for, and will, in and of itself, get you quite a lot of marks. But if you want to get top marks you'll need to *answer* the questions that you have been astute enough to raise. That's where your understanding of the topic and your revision will come into play.

How to write an essay: Writing the introduction

The introduction is the most important part of the essay:

- It is the first thing the examiner will read, and so will crucially influence her assessment of your work
- It is the springboard for and foundation of the rest of your essay

What will the examiner be looking for?

- **A genuine attempt to start to engage with the question**. (Contrast candidates who merely write out all they know about the topic, or who writing out some other - different - essay that they have memorised).
- She will also want to see that you have **a clear idea of where you are going** in this essay, a clear sense of the direction that your argument will develop in.

Writing the first sentence or two

The first sentence or two can be approached in a number of different ways:

- **One way is to comment on the specific words used in the question**. Talk about what those particular words imply. So, for example, with the Baldwin question, we could say something like, *"The question's use of the term 'Conservative success' assumes that the Conservatives were in fact successful, an assertion that will be examined below."* Or *"The question's use of the word 'extent' acknowledges that Baldwin was not the only factor promoting the Conservatives' dominance towards the end of the 20s"*.

- **Alternatively, say why this question in particular is interesting or important**. So, you might say, *"This question raises the interesting issue as to whether the personality of Baldwin himself was responsible for Conservative success, or whether there were other broader factors that led to the Conservative Party's electoral dominance"*.

The thing that the examiner will like about both these approaches is that they are **both saying something about the question** from the very first sentence.

CLASSIC MISTAKE: One common mistake here is that of starting to waffle about "background" or "context". **Just start to engage with the question from the very first sentence of the essay.**

Advantage of this approach: The great thing about commenting on the question is that it actually gives you something to say. Rather than your trying to formulate some general waffle, the wording of the question actually gives you something very concrete to work with. The brilliant thing is that, as well as being quite a straightforward thing to do, this is precisely the sort of stuff that the examiner loves to hear!

The next step: Telling the examiner what your argument is going to be

Having demonstrated to the examiner that you are in fact engaging with the question, the next step is to tell her, very briefly, about the general line of argument you are going to take.

Here are the magic words: The best way to do this is to signpost what you are doing to the examiner, by using the magic words: *"This essay will argue that..."*. Using this little phrase shows the examiner that you are actually planning on putting an argument together here. It tells her that you are not simply going to splurge out "everything you know about X".

So, in the Baldwin essay, you might say: *"This essay will argue that Baldwin's personal contribution to Conservative success was very significant, but that broader economic factors and the political weakness of the opposition parties were even more important."*

The phrase *"This essay will argue that"* is extremely powerful. You need to have an argument. You need to have a sense of direction as to where this essay is going. The magic phrase "this essay will argue that" gives you both an argument and a sense of purpose.

> You need to sound confident and have good
> essay style and structure. Albertine

Confident expression: Don't use phrases like "in my opinion" or "I think that maybe..". Expressions like these make you sound uncertain and vague, and will incline the examiner to think that you're not really sure what you're talking about. Every essay you write is your opinion, just as every essay is an expression of what you think, so you don't need to remind the examiner that this is the case. Just spit it out!

The final step: Setting out the structure of your argument

So, you've told the examiner what your overall line of argument is going to be. Now you need to show the examiner, briefly, a very clear outline of where you are going in the essay. Tell her about the things that you are going to discuss in order to move your argument forward. Don't tell her exactly what you are going to be arguing in each section – that's for the main bulk of the essay, and you don't have space to do that here. Simply outline the areas that you will be discussing in order to set out your argument.

The way that I do this, after setting out my argument, is to use the following phrase:

"This essay's argument will be structured as follows. First, ……. Secondly, ……. Thirdly, ……… Fourthly, ………. Fifthly, ……….. In conclusion we will consider…"

> *I always do like answers that say in the introduction 'there are five main points in answer to this question' and then follow them through in order in the rest of the essay. Simplicity of structure like this can actually show you have a real command and control of the subject matter.*
>
> *Jeremy*

Creating a positive impression: If you can set out your argument as clearly as this, it creates a very positive impression, and creating an impression is good when you consider that the examiner has 100 other exam scripts sitting beside her.

Mechanical can be good: The method outlined above is how I wrote my introductions in every single essay. Yes, it is a little bit mechanical, but it also produces very good introductions. Mechanical can be good because you know what you need to do and how you are going to do it. In the time-pressured environment of an exam you need a simple and effective method that you can rely on.

Get down to business: In an exam don't agonise too much over the first couple of sentences. Yes, think about them, but it is important to get stuck in and to not waste time. If you are talking about the question and engaging with it, you really cannot go too far wrong.

Keep it fairly brief: The introduction is important, but don't let it become too long. You need to get stuck in to answering the question properly in the body of the essay.

Emergency measures: Sometimes you will find yourself in difficulties, and even after some planning you may not be sure what your argument really is. In this situation leave a space for your introduction and then write it at the end by which time you will hopefully have a better idea of where your argument is going.

How to write an essay: Writing the body of the essay

Get stuck straight in to answering the question directly: Forget about "scene-setting" or "background" – it's very easy to get bogged down in this type of general waffle. The examiner can only start giving you marks once you start answering the question, so get on with it immediately.

Keep thinking about the question: As you begin each paragraph, think about the question again. Maybe even re-read it. Then, in the first sentence of each paragraph, engage with the question again. Refer to the wording of the question. Make use of the words that the examiner has used in the question. This will really show the examiner that you are sticking to that question like glue.

Don't worry too much about "both sides of the argument": Some people tend to get obsessed with the idea that you have to set out "both sides of the argument" before choosing which you prefer in the conclusion. My advice is to just answer the question. This is what the examiner has asked you to do. When answering the question, by all means show awareness that there are two or more sides to a particular argument. But don't let this get in the way of your simply getting stuck in and answering the question. You can briefly refer to the other side of the argument and briefly dismiss it.

So in practice you might say: I think ABC for reasons DEF – some other people think XYZ, but their argument is weak because of P and Q – therefore I think that ABC is a stronger argument.

Outcome: By playing it this way, you have shown awareness of the other position, while still being very clear what you think yourself. (This point is discussed in more detail on p 119).

What is a paragraph? A paragraph is a point. Each paragraph should make one big point - it should contain one idea, and should develop that idea. So: make your point, make it clear what you mean exactly, and then back it up with relevant facts and evidence. Bingo – you have just written a convincing paragraph!

Signposting: The first sentence of each paragraph should "signpost" the examiner by giving him a clear indication of what this paragraph is going to be talking about. Examiners need to read the essays quickly, so help them.

Length of paragraphs: A paragraph could be six lines or twenty lines. There are no precise rules here. Take as little or as much time as is needed to make the point that you want to make.

Get straight to the point: There is often a certain brutality about a good exam essay. In an exam you simply don't have the time to express yourself with as much elegance as you might otherwise. Express yourself directly, ruthlessly, and effectively. Just say it - this isn't a poetry competition!!

How to write an essay: Writing the conclusion

The conclusion is your chance to answer the question *in the light of the discussion that you set out in the main body of the essay.*

Before writing the conclusion, quickly read the title of the essay again, and take a few seconds to get it absolutely clear in your mind what your argument has been throughout.

When writing the conclusion's first few sentences:

- Use some of the words in the question to show that you are addressing it directly.
- Use phrases like "this essay has argued that". Underline the point that you have been answering the question by putting together an argument, rather than just aimlessly writing everything that you know about that particular topic.

- Refer to your earlier discussion of particular issues earlier in the essay.

So, for example, you might say "Baldwin's reforms of the Conservative Party's electoral machine, as argued in detail above, were the most important reasons for Conservative electoral success during the late 20s and early 30s".

The final sentences of an essay can be approached in a variety of ways:

- **Ram home your argument:**　Restate your main argument and underline the point that you have answered the question.　Use these sentences to make it very clear what you think.

- **Take a step back:**　Set what you have written in context.　The Baldwin question could be set in the context of how the Conservative Party had fared in the first part of the twentieth century, for example.　You could make some reference to the Conservative Party more generally in the aftermath of the First World War.

- **Give a personal view**:　For most of the essay there is no need to say "in my opinion" because the whole essay is in fact your opinion. However the conclusion is the exception to this rule.　Drawing attention to the fact that something is your personal view may make the examiner give you credit you have really been thinking about this for yourself and coming up with your own take on things.

- **Refer to the question:**　The best endings will often explicitly refer to what has been asked in the question, and to its specific wording.

- **Language:**　Generally speaking it is good to keep your language simple and concise.　However in the final sentences of an essay it can be good to use language that is a little more expansive and colourful, in order to finish memorably and with something of a flourish.

Example: So, for example, you might conclude, "Stepping back, and having considered Baldwin's reforms to key areas of Conservative electoral strategy, one might conclude that in doing so he laid the foundations for Conservatives' considerable successes in what remained of the twentieth century"

This concluding sentence refers to the question, sets the answer's significance in a broader content, and also gives a sense of Baldwin's activities as fitting into the broader sweep of history.

Essays at school – Helena's thoughts

For me, all arts essays at school had the same answer: Yes, No, Maybe.

The questions nearly always involved some kind of sweeping statement, be it: 'Was Charles I responsible for the outbreak of the Civil War in 1642?' or 'Without the soliloquies we have little understanding of Hamlet's state of mind'. Do you agree?

The answers could always follow the YES, NO, MAYBE pattern: e.g.

- *YES, Charles was responsible for the outbreak of civil war in 1642 for these reasons - blah blah blah...*
- *but NO, on the other hand there were other causes, we can't blame Charles for blah blah and blah...*
- *so overall MAYBE, he was quite responsible, but not totally. Overall I'd blame blah blah blah...*

Same with Hamlet:

- *YES the soliloquies provide us with a crucial insight into his state of mind - e.g. in these examples blah blah.. ..*
- *and yet NO, we can still understand his state of mind from other parts of the play, for example blah blah and blah...*
- *so overall MAYBE: the soliloquies are certainly important but they're not everything...*

It's not sophisticated but it's a useful way of getting started, especially at school when it might be the first time you've been asked to structure an essay. It's a really helpful way of making you order your thoughts, and to help the reader follow through a logical argument.

Questions of extent: As Helena points out, A-Level essays are often questions of extent. The question suggests one factor, and the answer lies in setting the importance of that factor within the context of a number of other relevant factors, and in so doing to assess its weight. The same point applies to the Baldwin question discussed above. Baldwin's contribution to the success of the Conservative party could only be accurately assessed in the context of other possible factors. Make sure you choose which of these factors is the most important so that you don't get accused of "sitting on the fence".

Advanced essay-writing: Argument vs Balance

What's coming up: In this section I'm going to go into a bit more detail on some of the issues that we touched on earlier. What follows will be especially useful for students in the later years of university. (Fast forward to the section on writing (p 108) if this isn't going to be much use to you).

The question I want to consider here is this: if two or more authors have different opinions on an issue, then what should I do? Do I set out their positions and then decide between them in the conclusion? Do I set out their opinions and evaluate them as I go along? How should I approach this?

There are a number of different aspects to what you have to do here:

Answer the question set: You'll remember that I've been saying to answer the question, but this point is a little bit different.   Generally speaking the examiner will be asking about what *you* think, not about what any one particular academic author thinks.   However, discussing what particular authors think may be helpful in explaining what you think i.e. you might *agree* with Smith or do you *disagree* with Smith, and *why*?

Give a personal evaluation of other people's arguments: Just telling the examiner "Smith says X" will certainly get you some credit. But you will take your answer to a much higher level if you not only wheel out Smith's argument, but then actually go on to **evaluate** it. So, you could say "Smith says X, and I think this is plausible because of Y and Z". Produce evidence to support what you think.

Compare one academic's views with another: If Smith says X but Jones says Y then in the course of answering the question you can outline their positions and say which is the better argument and why. Examiners will love this because it *"shows awareness of current debates"*. There are areas of controversy at the cutting edge or frontiers of every subject, but many weaker students will be unaware that they exist at all. The examiner may well have set the question with a certain academic debate in mind, testing whether or not you are aware of it, and offering you the chance to participate in it by setting out the answer as YOU see it, in the light of that debate.

Show that you are thinking for yourself: Particularly at university level, lecturers will be keen to see you demonstrate independent thought, so go ahead and make your own judgements. They will want to see that you are not only aware of the cutting edge debates in their subjects, but like to see you actually participating in them. Every essay is "in your opinion" so you don't need to keep pointing this out. *However* using this phrase when evaluating other people's contributions can usefully draw attention to your capacity for independent thought.

Showing awareness is not the same as being even-handed: There is an art to this - briefly show awareness of Jones' contribution, but then swiftly rubbish it by referring to a key piece of evidence that he has inexplicably overlooked. Then return to the main business of setting out your own answer to the question at hand.

You must have an argument: Before going into the exam you need to have worked out what you think about the big issues that the course has dealt with. You need to have a broad view on any issue that might come up, so that you know where you stand and can argue strongly.

Broadly agreeing with an existing view: Your argument may well be very similar to that of some major participant in the debate whose views you have read. You may find what they say convincing. *Adopting the position of one of the main participants in the debate, and drawing on their analysis, is generally an accepted way of going about things.* Few students are likely to be able to come up with better ideas than Professors who have spent their whole lives thinking about these issues. If your argument draws heavily on one particular author, then in the exam you can put in brackets "(drawing on the analysis of Finnis)" to show your awareness of this. In coursework remember to cite the person you are following otherwise it's plagiarism (see p 116).

When you are making your notes, put them together in the order that you will be using them for in the exam. Anticipate the argument that you will be putting together (I think X, which is the same as Smith, but incidentally Jones thinks Y which is wrong because of this piece of evidence E, so therefore X). Learn them in this order so that you can produce this argument more easily.

Express your views forcefully: If you think that someone's position completely misses the point, then say so very directly. Say that their argument is "simply not plausible" or that they have "overlooked the crucial point that..." (etc). The examiner will appreciate your lively writing style, and the very fact that you are confidently taking a position on the issue at hand will show that you have done some genuine thinking of your own about it (just as they will have done themselves).

Back your views up with evidence: It doesn't really so much matter *what you are arguing*, as long as you are *putting together a good argument*.

Don't sit on the fence until the conclusion: It is often thought (mistakenly) that academic essays have to give equal importance first to one side of the argument, then to the other, and then finally say which side you prefer in the conclusion. This is the surest and most boring path towards a mediocre result. It looks like you are sitting on the fence. Come down hard on one side of the argument from the very beginning of the essay. Start answering the question, and arguing the case for the particular answer you are putting forward, right from the very beginning.

Appreciate complexity, but make a choice: Often in reality there is more than one factor involved in explaining why something happened. This is particularly so in questions of extent, like the Baldwin question we looked at above. It can be difficult to put your finger on any one reason in particular that caused the outcome you have been discussing. But in these situations you should still just make a choice and say which factor you think was the most significant, and way. Saying something definite looks more convincing.

Take a stand: Take a position and argue this rigorously, backing it up with evidence (and rubbishing the other side of the argument) along the way.

In short: Forget balance - just answer the question. But in answering the question show awareness of the contributions of those misguided souls who don't think the same as you do.

However: If it turns out that the person marking your work wants to see a different approach, then give them what they want. Some lecturers, for example, simply like to hear their own views fed back to them. Find out which hoops they want you to jump through, and then head enthusiastically towards them.

Advanced essay-writing: Originality vs Independent Thought

To what extent do examiners at university want to see originality?

Is originality always good? It is often assumed that "original" is the same as "good" — that any "original" idea is by definition considered by the examiners to be a good thing. However "original" thought is good *only if* as well as being new, it is also both accurate and interesting. There is a very fine line between originality and just being plain wrong, or just saying something stupid. To illustrate this point with an extreme example, the idea that the Leaning Tower of Pisa is leaning because one side of it is made out of marshmallow is an *original* thought, sure, but it is also complete nonsense.

The difficulty of achieving useful originality: Originality that is in both accurate and interesting is extremely difficult to achieve. On any given topic there are Professors who are much cleverer than you or me and who have spent their *entire lives* thinking about this stuff. Over the course of a few weeks or even a term it is pretty unlikely that we are going to be able to come up with much that hasn't already been thought of.

Independent thought: What lecturers and examiners at university really want to see, I think, is evidence of independent thought, rather than originality. They want to see that you are sufficiently knowledgeable about and involved in the subject to the extent that you are really thinking about it for yourself and forming your own views. However these views don't have to be original with a capital "O". Instead you have looked carefully at the contributions of Professor X and Professor Y, thought hard about all the evidence available, and then decided that Professor X is probably right on the basis of the evidence (a), (b), and (c), that Professor Y is wrong because of (d) and (e), but that he does have a good point on (f). Your fresh take on the debate shows independent thought and is originality of a kind. It will certainly get you excellent marks. But it's not quite the same as the impossible task of being expected to come up with brilliant new theories of your own.

Advanced essay-writing: Making connections

Making connections will allow the examiner appreciate that you have a real understanding of the context of the answer that you are giving, and that you have been creatively thinking for yourself about these issues.

What types of connections are we talking about?

Connections with the broader themes of the course: So, you might be studying Hitler, but the broader themes or concepts of the course might be "European dictatorships", or "parallels and contrasts between the far right and the far left" or "the political uses of propaganda". How should you make this connection? Just say it. "My answer on this point connects with the broader issue of XYZ."

Connections with other courses in that subject: How does this term's work relate to last term's?

Connections between subjects: Draw on relevant understanding from other subjects. So, for example, if you are analysing a source question for history (e.g. a propaganda poster), then why not use some of the language-analysis techniques that you have picked up studying poetry and other English literature? Alternatively, if you have read literature from a particular period it may give you something more to say about its political developments. Academics love this sort of connection because it is "inter-disciplinary".

Connections with current events: Draw parallels with events that you have come across in the news. Read a quality newspaper or current affairs magazine (p 109) so that you have the information to do this. Be careful here, though - make sure that the parallels are subtle and take the time to explain exactly why you think that they are relevant. Don't say "Hitler was just like Saddam Hussein". You need to explain why the parallel is both (a) justified and (b) interesting - and so worth making in the first place.

Advanced essay-writing technique: Primary sources and arts subjects

In subjects like English Literature and Ancient History, really detailed knowledge of and engagement with the actual texts and pieces of evidence being studied is often key. What they're interested in is how familiar you are with the evidence and materials that form the very basis of the subjects that you are studying e.g. the actual works of literature that you are studying, as opposed to what other people have said about them.

> When I was studying Ancient History it was only about halfway through the course that I

realised that knowing all about the ancient sources was pretty much all they were interested in. They weren't interested in theories about what happened, but instead they wanted to know what we could say on the basis of the evidence (inscriptions, archaeological finds, literature from the time – that kind of thing). Actually, if I'd been listening carefully to what my Professor had been saying, he had mentioned this idea from time to time right from the very beginning of the course. From that point onwards I tried to back up every single thing I said with a reference to the primary sources, and I started doing a lot better! Matt

Give them what they want: Different tutors may like to see different things. It's possible that some might prefer the more theoretical approach. What they are looking for may be different to what you are think, so keep an open mind.

Find out what they want: Have a chat with your tutor early in the course to ask them what they want to see, and about which mistakes are commonly made. Get as much feedback as possible on each bit of work that you hand in so that you start to give them what they want sooner rather than later.

General points about writing

How you express yourself on paper will be a key factor in determining your grades. If you write well it will make a huge difference to the examiner's overall impression of your work.

Here is how to write well:

Keep it simple: Just Say It! Simplicity and clarity of expression is the name of the game. Don't try to think of some special or complicated way of putting your point across. Don't think that you have to develop some sophisticated "style" to impress the examiner. Just spit it out!

Short sentences are good: In sentences that are too long the meaning often becomes unclear. Overly long sentences are often the product of someone having started a sentence without really having a good idea as to what they want to say. If you don't know what you are saying, the examiner won't either.

Avoid fancy sentences, especially long ones: For one thing they will make you look pretentious. For another they are liable to go completely wrong. Orwell called this "purple prose". As soon as you find yourself writing a sentence that you feel a little too pleased about then stop immediately and stroke it out. You are probably trying too hard and the meaning is likely to be unclear. It is much more difficult, and more impressive to the examiner, if you manage to make your points clearly and succinctly.

> It takes far more effort and intelligence to convey a complex idea in a simple sentence than to convey a complex idea in a complex sentence. Someone who conveys simple ideas with complex sentences runs the risk of being considered pretentious. Dumb people are impressed by complexity and big words. Smart people are impressed by complexity conveyed simply. Kirk

Understanding is key: You will only be able to express yourself simply if you have a really good understanding of what you are talking about in the first place (See Chapter 10).

Spelling and grammar make a huge difference to the impression that you create. If you make a lot of mistakes then the examiner will assume that you are of lower ability no matter how good your content is. See the lists of common spelling and grammar mistakes at the back (p 218).

Vocabulary: While it is important to keep things simple, if you are familiar with some sophisticated words, and use them correctly, this can create a positive impression. But you must use them correctly - if you try to use a "big word" and get it wrong, you will look pretty stupid. However using a sophisticated word (correctly) can allow you to express ideas more succinctly than you might otherwise be able to.

Broaden your vocabulary generally so that you can express yourself more clearly when you're doing an exam:

- Get a **dictionary** and make use of it.
- Reading a **quality newspaper** or current affairs magazine can help with this. Some of these are free online. "The Economist" is the classic magazine for politics and world affairs.
- **Science magazines:** Your school library will probably have copies of them.

Never let a unknown word go by. If you come across a word you don't know look it up in the dictionary. Kirk

A lively writing style is a great asset: Putting your points across forcefully helps to convey the idea that you are making an argument, and makes it more interesting for the examiner. How to do this?

- Short sentences
- Phrases like "the fundamental point here is this: ..." The correct use of colons and semi-colons can be very effective (see p 223)
- Rhetorical questions: "How best to write persuasively? Let me explain."

Write in the active voice! "The man ate the sandwich" is simple and direct; "The sandwich was eaten by the man" requires two more words to express the same concept which is just stupid and kills any energy and momentum in the sentence. Kirk

Avoid the following:

- Abbreviations like "don't" and "isn't". I have used them a lot in this book to make it an easy read. But the examiner doesn't want to see them.
- Slang
- Starting sentences with the word "because".
- Over-use or over-repetition of certain words, e.g. "Basically, ...".
- Exclamation marks. Use them sparingly.
- Underlining
- Words entirely in capital letters.
- Jokes - if the examiner has marked eighty scripts by the time she gets to yours, she will have lost her sense of humour.
- Sweeping statements e.g. "Stalingrad was the most ferocious battle of the twentieth century". It's too easy to come up with counter-examples, and the fact that they are so general means that they aren't ever really telling the reader that much.

Essential points:

- ✓ Essays aren't just testing what you know: They're testing whether you can apply what you know to the specific question asked.
- ✓ Answering the actual question asked is the absolute key: Classic mistakes here include (1) writing everything you know that's vaguely relevant, and (2) wheeling out an answer that you have prepared to a different question.
- ✓ You will only be able to apply what you know to the question if you actually genuinely understand the material.
- ✓ *Introductions:* (1) Discuss language used in the question (2) Say what your argument is going to be "This essay will argue that.." (3) Set out the structure of the argument that you are going to follow – First, secondly, thirdly.
- ✓ *In the main body of the essay* each paragraph should make and develop one single point, backed up with evidence.
- ✓ *Conclusions:* Refer to the question. Be very clear as to what you think.
- ✓ Advanced essay-writing: Don't worry too much about balance – just answer the question. Evaluate other people's arguments. Originality is less important than demonstrating independent thought. Primary sources may be more important than you think.
- ✓ Writing: Keep it simple. Spit it out!!

6

Coursework and presentations

What's this chapter about?

Doing well at coursework is massively important to your end result, not least given that it's an increasingly popular method of assessment.

This chapter deals with the following issues:

> ➢ Choice of question
> ➢ Finding out what they want
> ➢ How to write a longer piece of work
> ➢ Plagiarism and referencing
> ➢ Presentations – how to do them

Coursework: General thoughts

- **You simply must do everything you can to nail it:** Coursework is a priceless opportunity to give yourself a little bit less to do in the exam in order to get the grade you want. You usually have plenty of time to do the coursework and you simply have to make sure that you do it well.

- **HOWEVER be careful not to spend too much time on coursework**: If the coursework is only worth, say, 20% of the overall result, there is a real danger that you spend too much time trying to make your coursework perfect, when it would be much more effective to use this time preparing for the exam. (The reason being that it's so much better to get an extra 5% in the exam than to get an extra 1% from the coursework).

Coursework: Choice of question

- **Make the work you do count double: ** If at all possible choose a topic that you will also be able to write about in the exam ****Don't do the coursework on something that is completely or largely irrelevant. You want the coursework material and the exam material to overlap, so that your work counts double. DON'T WASTE WORK!

I always did large amount of preparation for each essay because all the work I did for them I could also use for the exams. Kelly

- **Choose the difficult question:** If you have a choice of questions, and want to really impress, then go for the most challenging one. The more difficult the question, the more scope there will be for scoring extremely highly.

- **Ask for a different question:** If you are not happy with the questions on offer, make up one of your own and see if the tutor will agree to it. Try to create a question that will overlap with your preparation for the exam.

Coursework: Finding out your tutors' preferences

Coursework is different to exams, because with coursework the examiner is usually your teacher or lecturer. You therefore have a golden opportunity to find out exactly what they like to see and want to see in a piece of coursework that is presented to them. It is vital that you find out what they like to see, and that you do this BEFORE you hand in your coursework.

Remember the basic principle: We are interested in giving them what they want.

How do you do it? You just ASK them! Ask them what they like to see in the particular kind of work being assessed. Ask them what mistakes people commonly make. Ask them how you personally can improve on the basis of the work of yours that they've seen so far.

Marking framework: Your teacher may also have a sheet of the exam board's marking criteria for coursework. Ask them for a photocopy of this list. It is in both your interests for you to get a high mark!

What do they want to see?

- Some tutors love to *hear their own views* fed back to them: They may think that they know the "right answer", and want to hear it given back to them with a cherry on top.
- Other tutors are keen to *hear different views* or even to have their own views argued with.
- Different tutors *prefer different styles* e.g. most tutors don't want to see essays divided into subheadings, but the occasional tutor just loves to see this.

Which authors do they like? Ask your tutor who they think the best authors are on that particular subject. This will give you a great idea as to whose arguments and approach to follow in your own work. If a tutor says that they think Smith is a really great author, then chances are they will be happy to hear an argument that is broadly in line with what Smith thinks. But be careful to add some points from other authors or some of your own thoughts, otherwise it will be very obvious that you have just lifted your entire argument from Smith.

Advanced points: Finding out what they want

At university a number of further points apply:

- **Find out who is setting the exam and what they are interested in:** What have they been lecturing on? What have they recently been writing about? Look on their personal university page for clues.
- **Find out what the latest academic trends are:** Academically certain issues go in and out of fashion. Some topics are "hot topics" - the examiner is more likely to ask about these because they are interested in these issues themselves, and because they give the better students the opportunity to show off. Use Google to find out what the latest conferences in your subject have been discussing, and who has been speaking at them.

Coursework: How to write a longer piece of work

Choose your question carefully so that you can use that material for the exam and so that a good answer will really impress (p 114).

Find out what they want to see (Chapter 1).

Beat procrastination: Create momentum by doing just a little bit of the work required, and by breaking it down into smaller chunks (p 51).

Think about how you would answer the question before doing any of the reading: This forces you to consider what you actually know about the issue as it stands. It also forces you to look closely at the question, and particularly at its wording, which is of critical importance (p 89).

Get an overview so that you have some idea where you are going. Use a very simple textbook, Wikipedia, Google, or even children's books to do this.

Create a Master Document (p 70). Write the question you are trying to answer at the top. This will save you time by focussing your efforts on actually answering the question at hand.

Carefully choose a book you can get detailed notes from: These notes will provide the basic framework of your notes on this topic (your "Master Document") (p 68), and can then be supplemented by other reading. Use Amazon and Google to find the best book to use for your framework notes. Take these notes effectively as described in (Chapter 4). Remember to reference where you have got these notes from so that you don't get them confused with later additions (p 126).

Take the time to understand your framework notes: Actually knowing and understanding the material you already have will mean that you don't waste time covering the same ground later on. You will need to actually understand this material in order to answer the question anyway, so it's vital that to begin the process of understanding as early as possible.

Slot in other notes from further reading, lectures, etc. Synthesise these notes with your main notes in your "Master Document". Think about them and how they apply to the question as you are going along.

Use book reviews: They may save you reading the book itself, as they often summarise its key points. Crucially they are usually written by someone who knows a lot about that topic, which can really put the whole issue into context for you. You can usually find them in journals.

Blitz a few indexes: Towards the end of the writing process get hold of a few books and just totally blitz a few of their indexes. You're not looking to follow their entire arguments but rather just to get a few good nuggets of information that you can use to decorate your work. Spend just half an hour finding juicy examples and details, and then another half hour integrating these new points.

Do your coursework well in advance: Often your best ideas take time to emerge. Leaving coursework to near the hand-in date will not allow your mind enough time to work on it.

Planning is key: Put your notes away and write the question on a blank sheet of paper. Think about your answer to the question in the simplest possible terms. Try to come up with the simplest possible structure for your essay, one that flows from the question asked, and that answers it directly. See Chapters 5 and 10, on Essays and Understanding respectively, for more on how to do this.

Carry a pen and paper with you at all times so that you can jot down any ideas that occur to you. Your subconscious will be whirring away even when you're not at your desk, and it would be a shame to waste any useful "understanding" thoughts that arrive when you are out and about. Alternatively note things down in your phone. Keep a pen and paper beside your bed so you can write down any ideas and then get off to sleep. Later add these thoughts to your "Master Document" (p 70).

Thinking: Don't get bogged down with reading – it's the thinking that will really make the difference. Breadth of reading is less important than depth of understanding. Don't make the mistake of thinking "I'll do all the reading and then do all the understanding at the end" – you have to keep trying to understand the material as you're going along.   Attack the question (p 90). Some of the most valuable work you do will be carried out while your mouth is full of toast and you're staring out the window, or when you're talking with your Mum. Have a look at Chapter 10 on Understanding and also at the revision techniques in Chapter 11.

Don't write it immediately: One of the cleverest guys I know always played a game of squash after doing the reading for but before sitting down to write an essay. Give your subconscious a bit of time to sort things out in your head.

> *Often I find having some time for real distance and reflection from what you have been learning really helps, at the time it's often such a drive just to get all the key facts and arguments right that there's not time to properly process in your own mind as to what it all means. Paul*

"How to write the perfect essay" See Chapter 5.

Writing your paper:

- **Don't start writing until you know what you are going to say:** Don't use writing as a means of working out where you are going, as much of the actual writing itself will be a waste of time. Just do the thinking instead! The writing comes at the very end of the process.
- **It's a feel thing:** There will come a point when you just know that it's time to get this thing written.
- **Just let it out:** If you have done the planning properly then the writing will be the easy bit, as most of the information should be in your head. Ideally you will hardly need to look at your notes when you are drafting your answer.
- **Go with the flow:** If the drafting is going well then try to keep up momentum and complete the draft in one long work session. Ideally

you will only need to look at your notes again when it comes to doing the referencing. Leave all the referencing until the end – you don't want it to disrupt your train of thought or the development of your argument.

- **Keep it tight:** Keeping your work within the word count is almost always an issue, so write your draft in quite a compact style (good planning will help you here). Be careful you don't "talk to yourself" and then write it down. e.g. "Well we've just discussed x, but now it's time to start discussing y " – this is a waste of words, and one which you will end up having to delete to fit into the allocated word count.

- **Follow the leader:** When making certain points, writing certain paragraphs, or even when constructing your answer as a whole, you may well be following the argument of an author or academic whose position you find convincing. Remember to acknowledge the other side of the argument (even if only to dismiss it) and remember to personally evaluate their contribution in the light of the evidence (p 102), but - above all - remember to reference it (p 126).

- **Read it out loud** to check for grammatical errors. Or get someone else to read it for you if they are willing. Some computers have a text to speech function that can help here.

- **Get feedback before handing it in:** If your tutor is willing to review the coursework before it is handed in properly, then you absolutely must make the most of this.

- **Get feedback after handing it in:** Many people don't, and so waste this valuable opportunity to learn how to do better next time. Ask for specific points - if your tutor says that it was "pretty good" ask him how you could have made it excellent (p 16).

Plagiarism

What is plagiarism?

Plagiarism basically means taking other people's work and pretending that it's your own.

So, you can't:

- Copy other students' work
- Lift stuff directly out of books without referencing that you have done so

Possible consequences that we are keen to avoid:

- **At university** if you plagiarise someone's work, you could well get chucked out altogether. Universities actually manage to catch a surprisingly large number of people doing this each year. There are computer programmes that spot it.
- **At school** if you get caught copying someone else's essay you will definitely get into serious trouble. However referencing is generally not required before you get to university.

What you need to do: If you are using a point you've taken from a book then put it in your own words – paraphrase it.

Referencing: Use a footnote or an endnote to indicate that you have made use of someone else's text here.

What about exams? Here plagiarism is not something that you need to worry about. Just answer the question. However, if you are using an argument that obviously belongs to someone else, then just say so "Smith argues that XYZ" or put the author's name in brackets after you make that point.

Presentations

Presentations are increasingly used as a means of assessment, but they're much less common than exams and coursework, and so many people are a bit nervous about them. Don't be!

The normal principles apply: Find out what they want to see, and then give it to them. Ask the person assessing you about what they like to see in a presentation. Find out what they like, and then do it!

Making use of technology: Microsoft PowerPoint® is specifically designed for giving presentations. It is quite easy to learn to use, and there are plenty of instruction videos available on the internet (search YouTube®). PowerPoint® allows you to create a presentation on a series of slides. You will be expected to make use of this programme in the world of work, so you may as well pick up the basics now.

How to do a fantastic presentation:

- **Keep it simple:** Don't try to put too much on any one slide. Make one big point per slide. Keep it brief, keep it moving.
- **Don't use too much text:** The words on the slide are there to back up what you're saying, not to say it for you. Don't use more than two fonts otherwise your presentation will not look smooth and professional.
- **Pictures:** PowerPoint® makes it very easy to include pictures of things that you find on the internet (e.g. by searching Google images). It's also easy to adjust the size and position of your pictures using the programme. Use pictures to illuminate the points that you have chosen to make, rather than using them just for the sake of it, which can become distracting.

Key steps towards a successful presentation:

Grab their attention at the beginning with a striking picture or quotation. Say why you find it interesting. "I thought I'd begin my presentation by showing you this picture of X. The thing that I notice about it is Y, and this ties in with Z, which is the main thing I want to talk about today". Using a visual aid in this way also takes the pressure off you by giving everyone something to look at.

Define what you're going to talk about: "The issue I'm going to discuss today is X. Right at the outset, it's worth being clear that we're talking about X and not Y". Clarifying what you are going to be talking about can be done partly by saying what you are *not* going to be talking about.

Set out your structure: This is key. Having a defined structure makes it really easy for people to follow what you're saying, demonstrates that you have thought carefully about the content, and gives the strong impression that you know what you are doing. Have a separate slide giving an overview of your structure. The simpler your structure, the clearer your presentation will be.

Have an argument: As when writing an essay, an argument gives you a sense of direction and a sense of purpose (See p 95).

Communication, communication, communication

Don't use a script: You're not reading out an essay here. Direct communication with the audience is key, and you won't be able to do this if you have every word pre-planned. However you should have a very good idea indeed about what you are going to say. Practice your presentation so that you get it right – preparation and practice are the two crucial ingredients of your success. HOWEVER if there is a serious risk that you might go completely to pieces then bring in an emergency script with the whole thing written out word for word so that all is not completely lost.

Don't speak too quickly: The classic mistake is to rush through it, but you end up speaking so fast that no-one can understand a word you're saying. Take your time.

Umming and erring: Many people doing presentations for the first time end up saying "um" or "er" quite a lot, or else use the same word or expression again and again ("basically", "you know", "obviously"). Make a recording of yourself giving the presentation to find out what you really sound like.

Eye contact: Make eye contact especially with the person who is marking your presentation. They will also be looking to see if you are addressing the room as a whole. Just pick someone you get on with on the other side of the room from the examiner and talk half to her and half to the examiner. Another way of doing it is to imagine that you are talking to a group of friends.

Addressing the audience: "Now, when first looking at this picture you might think, as I did, that ... ..." Addressing the audience directly personalises your presentation, and shows that you are communicating with and interacting with them.

Nerves: Nerves are totally normal and show that you want to do well. Have a look at the discussion of exam nerves later in the book (p 190). What are you thinking about while other people are presenting? That's right, you're thinking about what you're going to have for dinner. People don't really care about what you are saying, so just blast on with it and try to get as good a mark as possible.

Performance: Presentations involve an element of performance. Think of it as a piece of theatre, rather than as a reading from one of your essays. Give your presentation in this spirit. It's showtime!

Presentation Practicalities

- **Computer:** Make sure that the computer is sorted out in advance so that you don't have stressful IT difficulties.
- **Room:** Have a look at the room first to make sure that there are no problems and to get used to the place you will be giving the presentation in.
- **Timing:** Make sure that your timings are right – sort this out when you are practising.

Handouts: Creating a handout can be useful to give people an outline of your structure and some key facts. It also looks impressive that you have gone to this extra effort, and may get you a better mark.

Conclusions: How to wrap it up

- **Come to a definite ending** rather than fizzling to a halt. Tell your audience that you are now stepping back to review what's been said and to give a few closing thoughts.
- **Remind your audience** what you had said you would talk about, briefly touch on the different things you talked about, and then give your verdict.
- **Give them a "take home message"** by summarising your key points in a sentence or two. Have a slide to help you make these points.
- **Give your own personal judgement** to demonstrate independent thought (p 102). Say *"My personal view is that..XYZ"*.
- **Come full circle:** If you used a picture or quotation at the beginning of the presentation then come back to it and say something new about it in the light of your discussion. Doing this will look sophisticated because it gives that idea that things have come full circle.
- **Finally say "thank you very much for listening"** or "thank you very much for your attention", to indicate clearly that you have finished, so that everyone knows where they are. You've done it!

Referencing

What is it? Referencing is saying where you got particular ideas from. I personally hate it, for the record!

When do you do it? You need to do it if you are quoting directly from a book or article, and you should also do it even if you have put the material in your own words. You need to let them know where you got that idea from.

Why do you have to do it? At university if you don't say where you got your idea from you might be accused of plagiarism (p 121).

How do you do it?

- **Find out which style your university requires:** Different universities prefer different styles. For example, one popular method is "Harvard" referencing. Usually your faculty will have a "style sheet" explaining how to actually do the referencing style that they prefer. Alternatively use Google to find an explanation of what the style required involves.

- **When you are taking your notes** for a piece of work that you will need to reference, save time by referencing each note after you have taken them. My own method is to mark each note with a little referencing code:

  e.g.   (MG/RJ/44) – referring to "Martin Goodman" "Rome and Jerusalem" page 44.

  Just "cut and paste" the code you create, and then change the page numbers to mark where each note comes from. Keep track of your abbreviations by keeping a list of books you have read for that particular paper.

- **Save time by creating the following documents:**
  - o **A master referencing document:** When you are referencing your very first essay create a document that you can use to help you remember how to reference in your university's preferred style in every subsequent essay. So, if they want you to reference in the "Harvard" style for example, create an example of how this applies (a) to books, (b) to articles in journals, and (c) to articles within books both (i) in the bibliography and (ii) in the footnotes. This will mean that you don't have to work this all out from scratch each time you need to reference an essay.
  - o **Your referencing document for that particular essay:** In some essays you will end up footnoting a few particular books etc on a large number of occasions. Create a separate document with these books' footnote references so that you can easily "cut and paste" them without having to hunt around to find them the whole time.
- **Electronic referencing:** For longer documents there are computer programmes that you can use to help with referencing.
- **Style point:** If you have quite a number of references all to the same book but all in the same paragraph, then just reference it once at the beginning of that paragraph but say in the footnote that "this paragraph draws heavily on..." whichever book it is and refer to the full batch of pages (e.g. pp. 74-83).
- **Bibliography:** This is the list of books, articles and other material that you have consulted in order to write the essay. In some subjects you will have to list your primary material (e.g. "Primary Sources" in history) separately from your secondary material (i.e. modern academics' books and articles discussing that primary material). Make sure that you list where you found and the precise nature of that primary material (e.g. The Bible New International Version). Include material that you have found on the internet (but don't mention Wikipedia!). To save time you can cut and paste from the bibliography of other essays for which you used the same books. Make sure that you actually use or refer to every item that you

mention in the bibliography, otherwise it will look as if you are just adding them to look impressive.

- **When should I do the referencing?** Immediately after you have taken the notes from that particular chapter or series of pages then note down where they came from (p 68). When you are writing your piece of work you should leave the referencing until the very end, so that it doesn't distract you.

Essential points:

✓ Give coursework the time it deserves (but it's possible that this is less than you think!)

✓ Make your work count double by choosing a question that will also help you to prepare for the exam.

✓ Find out what they want! Ask about common mistakes and about what they like to see.

✓ Writing a paper: Take time to understand the work as you are going along. Planning is key.

✓ Presentations: Practice loads. Set out your structure at beginning. Keep it simple. Engage the audience. Take your time. Come to a definite conclusion.

Science: your formula for success

What's this chapter about?

This chapter contains material of specific use to readers who are studying science. But you have to read the rest of the book as well!!

The sections coming up deal with the following issues:

- How to think like a scientist
- Winning tactics for studying science
- Revising science subjects
- Exam technique (general tips for science exams)
- Exam technique (the different types of science exam)

Think like a scientist: Asking the right questions

Scientists are always wanting to prove things. They always want to know WHY something is the case. Why does it work that way? Why is it like that? Mathematicians and scientists will ask "why?" quite a lot. If you don't ask "why", then you are not really a scientist, I would say.

Graham

Keep digging. You have to keep digging one level deeper, all the time. Sachin

Scientists ask the questions "What" "Why" and "What If". All of science and Maths is based around answering these questions.

Emily

"What if" questions are another great way of improving your understanding. "What will happen if I change some component?" "What will happen if we block some step here?"

Think like a scientist: First principles and their uses

Spend time getting to grips with the most basic concepts of your topic. All the more complicated things are based on simple basic principles, e.g. "across the cell wall negative and positive charges are always balanced".

To make sure that you understand the principle, try and break it down into its very simplest terms. Try and have such a clear and simple understanding of the topic that you could explain it to your Granny.

Once you have the basic scientific principles in your head, you can use these to work out more complicated situations or concepts even if you can't immediately recall the answer. You can work out more complicated things by referring back to and applying these "first principles".

Contrast, for example, learning a foreign language, where if you don't know if a certain word is masculine or feminine you can't really work it out. You either know it or you don't. Or contrast history, where if you simply don't know what happened, it's difficult to say that much at all.

Science is logical. It all fits together and does so on the basis of first principles. The fact that science flows from first principles is the reason that it all makes sense. Emily

Doing well at science requires a rock solid understanding of the absolute basics. Sachin

Studying science: Do lots of problem questions

**The number one thing that will improve your ability is doing lots and lots of problem questions ** The friends I consulted for the writing of this chapter emphasised this point again and again.

> *You need to practise problem after problem to gain confidence and skills. So long as you're doing problems you'll get better. If you kid yourself that you've understood something without taking the time to check this by answering questions on it then you'll get into trouble. You need to spend weeks or even months practising questions, and years beforehand picking up formula and learning where to apply them. Graham*

Don't cheat: The danger here is that after finding the answer at the back you start to convince yourself that you've understood the problem, when you actually haven't. NOTHING replaces struggling through the problem. No pain, no gain!

> *Go through old exams and old problem papers to see what you did wrong, how you did well and WHY. Without understanding where you have made mistakes you won't really have moved on. You have to learn from your mistakes, otherwise you're not actually making any progress. Graham*

What you're trying to learn here: This isn't just about understanding how to do that particular problem. More fundamentally, it's about trying to grasp the underlying concepts. After each problem, write down what you learned from doing the problem - not the answer, but the principle or idea that you learned from doing it. When it comes to revision, review the list of principles alongside the problems themselves.

Use past papers as you are going along: There's no better way to find out if you have actually understood a topic than actually doing questions on it from a real exam.

Studying science: Participate in class

Learning science is not a spectator sport: Getting involved in solving problems in class is a much more effective way of learning than hanging around on the sidelines.

> I find that the best way to learn is by doing and by application. I always really learnt and understood stuff properly when I was applying it rather than when I was just learning it for its own sake. Iain

Lectures are key in science subjects. Preparing beforehand will mean that you get more out of them, reviewing afterwards will make you more likely to understand and to remember the ground you've covered (p 78).

Studying science: Don't fall behind

> If you don't understand something, there's a benefit of sleeping on it and trying to figure it out again when you're rested. But if you still don't have the slightest idea what is going on, and especially in subjects like Physics, Maths or Economics, then get help before you end up so far behind that you can't catch up to the class. It's far better to go through a moment of admitting that you're clueless than continuing to suffer and ultimately failing the exam. Kirk

In a subject like Maths one week's work often builds on that of previous weeks. So if you don't understand one thing, then this may stop you from understanding the next six things. Therefore if you don't get some help early on, you might end up in a state of permanent catch-up where the situation just gets worse and worse.

Sciences are accumulative in the sense that learning new stuff depends on understanding the material that you've covered already. So if you miss a key point early on in course then make sure you go back over it with the help of one of your pals or your teacher. Emily

Studying science: Making connections

There's a lot of overlap between the different science subjects, which you can use to your advantage.

Look out for overlaps and parallels between the different science subjects. *Allow yourself to form mental links across "separate" subjects – between mechanics in Physics and Maths; between Physical Chemistry and Physics; between Organic Chemistry and Biology, etc.*

Also look for links within the subject itself *– teachers / lecturers will have arranged their courses in the order they're in for a reason – once you've got the ideas move on, but watch for the same ideas being used later on. Iain*

Studying science: Thinking in different ways

Make it visual:

- **The power of the diagram:** Drawing pictures, diagrams or flow charts for every question makes you visualise what it's asking about and so makes you think about it from a different angle. Biology, for example, is a very visual subject, and any of the concepts are best explained as a picture.

- **Colouring books:** Use Biology and Anatomy colouring books to work with your visual memory. Books like this are great because they make you interact actively with the material. But use them only to supplement your other notes, rather than to replace them.
- **Visualise processes in action:** e.g. Imagine biological processes going on in your own body.
- **Google images:** Search Google's image library for flowcharts, pictures of the cell wall, metabolic pathways etc.
- **Photocopy** diagrams and pictures, label them, and include them in your notes.

Say it out loud: Describing a problem out loud can also help the process of understanding. Both these techniques makes your brain think in a different way!

Revising for science: Learning

Science subjects require a more intense form of learning than subjects like History and English Literature. In Arts subjects you can usually come up with something to say, but in a science exam, if you don't have a perfect grasp of a particular formula you need, you're completely screwed. Thinking from first principles can get you quite far, but there are some things that you just have to know.

Test yourself so that you are absolutely sure that you REALLY know it: Read about how to do this and about other learning techniques in Chapter 11 "How to learn stuff".

Revising for science: Problem questions

In science exams in particular, practise makes perfect. There is a limit to the number of ways examiners can ask scientific questions, so spend time doing as many past papers as possible so that you are able to easily recognise what principle they are testing in each question, you will get quicker at working through the problems, it will help you identify the things you have perhaps not entirely understood (or not perfectly memorised) and you will gain confidence in your ability to ace the exam. You don't need to be nervous walking in to a science exam once you have done all the past papers you can get your hands on, as there will be absolutely no surprises waiting for you. My best performance ever in an exam was in sixth year chemistry. I had done every past paper for the previous twelve years. In the exam it was almost as if I had seen it all before. It was like re-reading a favourite old story.

Emily

Revising for science: Learning how to get by

Even if you can't manage to completely understand a particular topic, you can still memories the technique of how to do questions in it:

Particularly at school level Maths, even if you don't completely understand the underlying concepts needed to solve a problem you can still get full marks in the exam simply by learning the method of how to approach that type of question. Just master the ingredients of what you have to do, learn the processes, and then follow them in the exam. It's far from ideal, as you don't get to understand it properly - but at least you can actually do what they're asking of you!

Iain

Exam technique: General points

Read over the whole exam before starting: At the back of your mind your subconscious will start working away at the more difficult problems.

Do the easiest questions first: There's always the danger of getting bogged down in the more difficult problems, and if you are under pressure of time even the easier questions will become more difficult. "Gather the low-hanging fruit!"

Read the question carefully and come up with a plan of how you're going to answer it: Don't rush into trying to solve a particular problem. First of all take the time to clearly work out what exactly the question is asking you, and what sort of problem it actually is.

Tackle problems step by step: Breaking large questions down into little pieces can make them more manageable.

Show your working out!

> When you're doing Maths make sure you show all your working out because you will get marks for this. Liz.

Showing your working out is vital because this is precisely how you get your marks.

Keep moving on! Don't get bogged down. You could be using that time to get easier marks in other parts of the exam. Treat the exam like a game, and maintain a positive attitude.

> If you get stuck then try leaving that question it and coming back to it later - Sometimes it will suddenly seem obvious what you needed to do in that question you've just moved on from. Helena

Expect the unexpected: In science and Math courses questions often combine the course's material in new ways. You are not expected to "know" the answers to these problems – the whole point of the exam is that you have to figure them out. To do so, think on paper as methodically as possible so that you leave a record of your reasoning.

"Reality check" your answers:

> *In exams you can raise your mark quite a lot by reality checking the answer and then checking back through if it makes no sense. Graham*

Under pressure in the exam it's easy to misclick on the calculator or to misplace a decimal point. So when you come to your final answer assess it from a common sense perspective. For example, if the question is about calculating the true length of a football pitch, and your answer is that it is 90,000 metres long then you must have taken a wrong turning at some point! 90m long would have been a much more plausible answer.

Exam technique: Short answer questions

> *Look at the bottom corner of the answer box, as there will often be a number showing you the number of marks that can be awarded for each question. This gives you an idea of how many specific points they are looking for you to make in your short answer. Judge how long you should spend answering that question on the basis of how many marks it's worth. Ellie*

When answering remember to separate out your points clearly. Make three short points separately, rather than running your points together in one jumbled paragraph.

> *If you don't know an answer to a particular question straight away, my advice would be to mark that question down on your piece of scrap paper, and move onto the next question. By the time you have answered a few more questions you may find that your 'subconscious' has dredged*

up the answer for you without you having to actively think about it too much! Ellie

Some science topics just come down to memorising for the day e.g. the Krebs cycle or any anatomy. Liz

Keep it brief: Don't write a sentence if a word will do. Find out (in advance) if they want you to write in full sentences or whether you can get away with single word answers.

Define terms: Demonstrate to the examiner that you are absolutely clear about the terms that you are using. This can get you marks in and of itself.

Exam technique: Multiple choice questions (MCQs)

1. Read the question carefully. Underline key words. Look out for unexpected negatives e.g. the following are NOT true. Look for clues in the question e.g. an indication that the answer will be in the plural.
2. Try to come up with the correct answer before you even look at the choices. Sometimes the options you are given are deliberately quite close, so avoid this potential for confusion.
3. Read the possible answers carefully, all of them, even if you see the right answer straight away.
4. Cross out the answers you know are incorrect.
5. Mark any questions where you are unsure of the answer so you can come back to them later. Use a star system to prioritise e.g. two stars for questions you really want to come back to, just one for questions that you'd just quite like to have another look at.
6. Remember that they are unlikely to be taking marks off if you get questions wrong ("negative marking"). If negative marking is being used, this will be absolutely clear on

the front sheet of the exam. If negative
marking is not being used then you have
nothing to lose by having a guess.
7. *Keep an eye on the time!*
   Ellie

Exam technique: Essays in science subjects

Don't let this be your Achilles' heel: Many science students are great at problem-solving questions but haven't had as much practice with essays. But if the essay component is worth 30% of the overall mark, it's seriously worth getting good at them.

Find out what they want: the basic principle still applies - you can only give them what they want if you know what they like to see. Ask your tutor and have a look at Examiners' Reports to find out what they're looking for. See Chapter 1 "Finding out what they want to see".

Define important terms: when introducing a specific scientific term that you are going to be using, explain exactly what you mean by it. This will make it clear to the examiners that you know what you are writing about. For example - ' *Homeostasis, the regulation of an internal environment to maintain a stable and constant condition, is essential for complex organisms to survive'.*

Structure your answer: although I choose not to put headings into my essays as I think this will limit me if I need to add anything extra at the end, I mentally do this and jot it down on scrap paper before starting my writing.

Think what they're looking for: What are they testing? What do they want to be sure I know?

Answer the question, with examples and evidence where appropriate. It's really important that you remember to back up what you say with **evidence.**

Are you going to use diagrams? Only use them if they are actually going to help to explain your answer. Don't start drawing them just for the sake of it.

In conclusion: Have a brief summary at the end. Try not to introduce any new information in the summary.

The importance of style: It's content that will get you the marks, but style will help your examiners to see where the content lies.

Keep it clear: Your examiner may well be marking hundreds of papers, under time pressure, and a muddled, unplanned answer may be brilliant, but is going to be a real pain to mark.

Keep it neat: Untidy writing and lots of crossing out and things written in the margin could mean that you miss out on marks. The examiner can't give you credit if it is impossible to see what you have written.

Keep it concise: Scientific writing is usually done in a more factual and concise way than essays in arts subjects like English Literature or History.

Ellie

Languages:

Say bonjour to better grades

What's this chapter about?

The skills involved in learning a foreign language are a bit different to those required for other subjects, so it's worth focussing on them separately.

This chapter's sections include:

> ➤ Four great ways to learn vocabulary
> ➤ Speaking and listening
> ➤ A few extra tips at the end

Four great ways to learn vocabulary

• **Learning vocabulary (1) – Use the power of your imagination:**

Example: The German word for bottle is "die Flasche". Here's how to remember it - the word "Flasche" sounds a bit like the English word "flesh", right? So imagine a bottle made of human flesh. Gross, but that's the point – it's memorable.

Taking it further: You could add to it - Flasche also sounds a bit like "flashing". So you can imagine a bottle made of human flesh flashing on and off like a light. Now you will never forget what the German word for bottle is!

Benefits: This approach makes learning vocabulary a little bit more fun, and is also more effective than the usual method of just staring at the page and hoping that it somehow goes in.

• **Learning vocabulary (2) – Learn sentences, not just words:**

Rather than just learning the word "le placard" (the cupboard), learn the sentence "il l'a mis dans le placard" (he put it in the cupboard). Why do it this way? Well, for one thing you are more likely to remember the vocabulary in a sentence because this is how we generally encounter words in real life. Secondly, you get to practice a bit of grammar along the way. Almost without thinking about it, here we have also revised the past tense and the positioning of pronouns. Thirdly, you may be able to learn several new words in the same sentence, which is especially good if they are words that might often be used together anyway.

- **Learning vocabulary (3) – Say it out loud:**

Saying the words and phrases that you are learning out loud will help them to stick in your memory.

- **Learning vocabulary (4) – Be selective:**

Don't try to learn every word. Learn the word for "cupboard" rather than the word for "propeller". Exam boards sometimes publish lists of the specific vocabulary that will come up in the exam.

Speaking and listening

- **Being good at these can make all the difference**

The speaking and listening components are often 50% of the total marks for languages exams at school. However these skills are often not practised nearly enough given the huge amount of marks riding on them.

Listening: Buy some CDs or DVDs off the internet and practice listening to them. Or listen to radio stations from that country – you should be able to get them really easily over the internet. In the exam, if you don't hear something properly then write down how it sounded in English so that you can come back to it.

Speaking: Try to find someone from that country who you can practice with a bit. In the exam pause for a second before answering the question. This won't lose you marks, but will gain you a little extra thinking time. Learn how to say "please could you repeat the question".

- **Participate in class:**

Actively participating in class will help you to remember a foreign language much, much more than just sitting back and allowing it to wash over you.

- **Pronunciation:**

Pay very close attention: Foreign languages may well use the same alphabet as us, but the pronunciation is completely different. Your speaking skills can only start to improve once you accept and start to look out for these differences in pronunciation.

EXAMPLE: Let's have a look at the word "cardinal" in French. It means the same as it does in English. It looks the same. But in actual fact each of its syllable is pronounced very differently:

- "car" is pronounced with the French "r" which is softer and throatier than in English. The "c" is also pronounced in a tighter and more emphatic way than it is in English.
- "di" is pronounced "deee" Tight and quick.
- "nal" is pronounced much more quickly and more tightly than you (as a native English speaker) might think.

The point is that the pronunciation of each and every syllable involved is in fact different.

Another example here is that the French word "tu" (you) uses a "u" sound that is much tighter and higher than we might pronounce it in English. Every language uses many sounds that simply do not exist in English.

Listen very carefully to how different words are pronounced, and then write down how each syllable is actually pronounced just above the word in French.

Also look out for where different languages place emphasis in different words.

EXAMPLE: "Bonjour". The classic mistake here is to place too much emphasis on the first part of the word: BON-jour. But if you listen carefully, you will notice that the French have an even distribution of weight between the two parts of the word: bon-jour. In practice this means that you (as a native English speaker) have to make a special effort to give more weight to this second part of the word.

A few extra tips

- **Grammar**

Accept that quite a lot of grammar is illogical and you just have to learn it.

- **Read something that you are interested in anyway**

If you're learning French and are interested in cars, why not read through a French car magazine online? You'll meet a lot of useful grammar and vocabulary, and will do so in a context where you are interested in and so more likely to remember the material.

- **Cramming doesn't work**

> *The night before a language exam you should be out playing tennis. You can't cram for this type of exam, you just have to do the work along the way. It's a bit like learning a musical instrument – you just can't do it the night before. Patricia*

9

The vital importance of

having fun

What's this chapter about?

I think you'll find this chapter quite refreshing, because it's about having the most fun possible. Why? Well because if you're not having fun, you're not going to perform as well as you can academically.

So this chapter's about quitting at the right time about and planning your leisure time so that you can maximise the time you have off, in terms of both quantity and quality. It's about taking time completely off rather than wasting your time in that grey area between work and relaxation. It's about getting proper sleep and doing some exercise so that you can work properly when you need to get back in the academic game.

It's also about making the most of the people you're surrounded by – by friends and family who will hopefully want you to do well, and who can offer the support and encouragement that can make all the difference.

Having more fun will get you better grades

MYTH: There's definitely a myth that people who get the best results spend their entire lives chained to their desk, with match-sticks propping up their eyes.

REALITY: Sure, if you want good results you are going to have to work pretty hard. But you can only give your work 100% if you are ready to concentrate and to give it your best shot. You need to be fresh, relaxed and ready to focus.

The art of finishing for the day

Avoid just going through the motions: Sitting at your desk but not achieving anything is a complete waste of time. There is only so much revision you can do in a day. Your brain is like a sponge that will only soak up so much information at a time. Pretending to work achieves nothing.

Don't look back: Your decision to stop must be final. Wondering whether you should go back and do another little bit will mean that you can't relax properly and so will simply ruin your time off.

Before stopping work the last thing you do should be to have a think about what work you will be doing tomorrow. Write this down to get it out of your head, so that you aren't thinking about what work you have to do next when you are supposed to be relaxing.

Planning for maxImum fun

What are we trying to achieve here? Having the maximum fun possible means that you will be motivated and have lots of energy when you sit back down at your desk.

CLASSIC MISTAKES:

- **Clicking your life away:** The worst thing you can possibly do is to keep sitting at your desk, mindlessly surfing the internet. We all know how easy it is for hours to slip by, clicking on this, clicking on that. But really, this is such low quality entertainment.
- **Watching random TV:** Just drifting downstairs to watch *random TV* is another classic trap. Recording your favourite shows, or streaming them over the internet, can be a great way of making sure that you are at least watching something you are genuinely interested in.

How to do it: Actively planning your leisure time will allow you to have more fun. Arrange to meet up with friends and go out somewhere. Planning something also gives you an event to look forward to when you are in the thick of work or revision.

Taking days completely off

Take at least one day completely off work each week. You need space to clear your head and time to unwind.

Take it COMPLETELY OFF: Don't say to yourself, "well, I wanted to take a day off but I'll just maybe do an hour at the books in the afternoon at some point". This doesn't work. That hour will be hanging over you all day, which will still feel like a work day, even though it is a precious day off. This is a disaster - you are wasting your own time by not making the most of your time off.

Decide the night before: Don't "See how you feel in the morning". In the morning you won't be sure, and you will waste half the day feeling uncertain and / or guilty before finally deciding to take the day off. The problem is that you've already wasted half of it thinking about work.

Have a regular day off: Having a regular day that you take off each week will mean that you don't have to waste time and energy constantly making this decision. It also gives you something definite to look forward to.

Take some weekends completely off during term if you can. One day completely off is good, but two is even better!

Plan ahead: There's nothing worse than wasting a day off by achieving little more than "faffing around". Planning helps you to make the most of your time, gives you something to look forward to while you are working, and it's a nice distraction to think about and to organise during your breaks.

Know yourself: Learn to judge how tired or otherwise you are feeling. Think about how many days you will need off to be in form and want to get back into the work on the other side of it. Learn how to manage yourself. This is not about being lazy, it's about being smart. It's about making the most of your leisure time, so that you are in the best position to make the most of your work time.

Take good chunks off during the holidays, especially Christmas and at Easter. Try to anticipate when you are going to become tired and take a holiday to avoid the risk that you start to mentally or physically run out of steam. You often don't realise how tired you are until after the first few days that you take off, when you really start to relax properly. Plan to take time off BEFORE you become so tired that you HAVE to take a break. You don't want to run out of energy and enthusiasm in the week before the exams.

It's also extremely important to take days off during a series of exams, in order to avoid burn-out (p 155).

Sleep and napping

Quality work is only possible if you are pretty well slept:

- **Nights:** Make sure you are getting enough sleep.
- **Getting to bed:** Stop working at least an hour going for bed so that your brain has enough time to slow down and to relax.
- **Pen and paper:** Keep these by your bed in case you have any work-related thoughts that are preventing you from getting to sleep. Jotting them down will get work out of your head.

Diet and sleep:

- **Coffee:** Be careful how much caffeine you drink, particularly in the evening, as this may help you from getting to sleep properly.
- **Caffeine:** Isn't just in coffee. Tea, energy drinks, cola drinks and other fizzy drinks also contain significant quantities. Caffeine is the first thing that doctors ask about when you say you're not sleeping.
- **Alcohol** will wreck your sleep and harm your prospects of doing any quality work the next day.
- **Sugary foods** will give you a rush of energy but you will feel very low on energy once the sugar rush runs out. **"Slow-release" foods** like wholemeal bread, muesli or oatmeal will give you the sustained energy you need.

- **Water:** Make sure you drink enough, as a major cause of tiredness is dehydration.

Taking a nap can be a great way of getting fresh for another burst of work. Winston Churchill was a great fan of the nap, saying that he found that it added several hours of productivity to each day.

Exercise

Exercise it will help you get better exam results, it's as simple as that.

Its benefits include:

- Feeling happier: exercise releases endorphins which make you feel happy. Scientific studies show that there is a direct link between exercise and having good mental health.
- More energy.
- Better sleep at night.
- Escape from work! When you are focussed on trying to beat your opponent in a game of tennis, you are not thinking about work.
- It's another way to spend time with your friends.
- Playing a bit of sport can also be.... fun!!

Fitting it in: Even when you are revising hard there will still be plenty of hours in the day when you are not at your desk. Make the most of them!

Create your team

Your family can help you get the results you want: Their support and encouragement can potentially make a huge difference. No two families are the same, of course, and it is impossible to generalise about how you should or should not interact with your folks. But you might be surprised at how receptive your Mum and Dad are to talking about work. After all, they're your parents and most parents simply want their kids to do well. Brothers and sisters can also be a valuable source of support, particularly older siblings who may have been through it before and have some useful tips to pass on along the way.

Don't underestimate how important this kind of support is in terms of maintaining motivation. If you want to get great results then there will be a serious amount of lot of work to do, and to have a few people, or even one person, cheering you on will make a huge difference. All those little conversations and encouragements really add up. Talking about something with your family will make it more likely to happen. Your family will give you encouragement and support. You will also be more likely to work hard to prove to them that you can do it.

Encouraging the people who encourage you: Given that support from your family can help you do well, it's definitely something that you should encourage. If someone asks you how the work's going, then answer them nicely, even if you're not 100% in the mood to do so. Don't snap or strop even if you're feeling grumpy.

Well-being during exam time

Manage your general well-being over the exam period so that you can achieve peak performance.

DANGER: There's a real danger of arriving at the exams exhausted. You can't afford to mentally or physically conk out halfway through your set of exams.

It's vital that you are feeling fit and raring to go when the examiner says "you may start now". So:

Before the exams: Take a day off two or three days before they start so that you have some energy in reserve.

Get out of town: Beat boredom by taking a day completely off and have a complete change of scene. Get on a train and go somewhere – the sensation of moving quickly in the opposite direction to work can be extremely therapeutic.

During the exams it can be a very good idea to take some days completely off, so that you don't turn into an exam zombie.

Sleep:

- o **What's your sleep pattern like?** If you've generally been working at night are you going to be alert for an exam at 9.30 am?
- o **Stockpile some Zzzzzs:** In the weeks and months before the exams make sure that you are getting enough sleep generally, so that you will still have some energy "left in the tank".

Naps: Napping directly after an exam can get you fresh to prepare for another exam if you have one the next day.

Food: Eating junk won't give you the fuel you need to perform at your best.

Exercise: Keep it up to burn off your stress.

Good habits: The best way to avoid stress around exam time is to have a balanced lifestyle in the first place. Continue with the good habits that you have already created rather than setting them to one side because you are "doing exams".

Essential points:

- ✓ Don't believe the myth that working hard means you can't have fun.
- ✓ Working effectively is possible IF AND ONLY IF you are having fun
- ✓ Plan your leisure time and take it completely off. You need to recharge your batteries to the max.
- ✓ Sleep and exercise are cornerstones of both productivity and good mental health.
- ✓ Cultivate supportive relationships both inside and outside your family.
- ✓ Create good habits that will serve you well when it comes to exam time.

10

Understanding

(if you read one chapter make it this one)

What's this chapter about?

Taking the time to actually understand the work properly is the absolute key to doing well at exams.

This chapter addresses the following three issues:

- why understanding is so important
- how to understand something
- the true nature of understanding

Why understanding is so important: Understanding and the nature of exams

Genuinely understanding the material is of absolutely crucial importance because of the true nature of exams.

** It is often thought that the purpose of an exam is to test how much you know about that particular subject. YES, exams are about how much you know about your particular subject. BUT they are not JUST about how much you know. Exams are ALSO testing how well you are able to apply what you know to the question that the examiner has set. Exams test the ways in which you are able to make use of what you know in order to actually answer the question in front of you **

What does this mean in practice? It means that learning the relevant material is not going to be enough. In fact, it's not going to be anywhere near enough. Decent factual knowledge of the material will get you a "B". If you want an "A" you have to know your stuff, but you also have to apply it correctly to the question at hand. And if you want be in the position to apply what you know to the question, then you have to actually genuinely understand the material.

What is the difference between LEARNING and UNDERSTANDING? Parrots can learn stuff. Understanding requires much more familiarity with the material. You need to have thought about the "hows" and "whys" rather than merely the factual "whats".

What does this idea of APPLYING what you know to the question at hand really mean? The point is this: If the question is phrased in a way that is even slightly different to the way you have approached the topic in class, then merely rhyming off material you have learnt by heart will not be enough. You need to be able to ADAPT what you know and apply it to the question actually set. You will only be able to do this if you actually understand the material. While the exam question set may be similar to a question that you have covered in class, good examiners will add a little extra twist to it, precisely to separate the stronger candidates from the rest of the pack. They want to see if you have the understanding and intelligence to adapt what you know to the question that they actually asked.

> Try to understand the topic and what's relevant – this will make it easier to adapt to "unexpected" questions in an exam. Kirk

CLASSIC MISTAKE: The classic mistake in exams is that of seeing a word or two that you recognise and then vomiting out everything you know about topic X. Genuinely understanding the topic allows you to avoid this, because it means that you can adapt what you know to directly answer the specific question that the examiner has actually asked. You will be richly rewarded for doing so.

"Snap!": Without understanding the material, the exam is reduced to one big game of "Snap", where you see a question and think "oh I know about that!", and then just vomit out anything that seems relevant. This reduces the exam to a memory test, but the problem is that, as far as the examiner concerned, the exam is not just a memory test: it is the opportunity to see both (1) what you know and (2) how you can apply what you know to the question.

> The most common failing in exams is the reliance on pure memorization rather than actually understanding the subject. David

Application in the exam: Applying what you have learnt to the question will probably require a little bit of chopping and changing. You may have to leave out certain bits of the material you have learned, or emphasise different bits. You will only be able to do this if you actually understand the material that you have learned. Simply having learned the material "by heart" will not give you the flexibility that this requires. You need to understand the material well enough to be able to actually <u>use</u> it in the exam to answer the question.

Understanding is of critical importance precisely because it will allow you to think in the exam, meaning that when you start writing you will be answering the question. When you pick up the ball, you want to be running in the right direction!

Why understanding is so important: Understanding and memory

If you have genuinely understood something then you will find it much easier to remember. You almost don't have to remember it, because you just know it - on some level you have already absorbed and accepted this material.   It is almost as if you know it already, but just need to "remember" a few of the details.

> *Scientists often talk about "going back to first principles", and thinking about the absolute basics of a particular issue.   If you can't totally remember something in an exam, you can often work things out from "first principles".   But you can only do this if you actually understand the "first principles" in the first place! Emily*

Why understanding is so important: Trying to understand something makes doing work more interesting

The more you understand something the more interesting it gets. And if you find the work interesting, your preparation for the exam will suddenly become a whole lot easier.

> If I have prepared well then before the exam it's like I can see the work in 3-D... I can just turn it round in my head. It's like being Professor Craig for just a short while.... you have the overview of the whole term's work inside your head, all at that one moment. Kirsty

Why understanding is so important: Understanding means that you know what you think

Taking the time to understand the material means that you will know broadly what you think about the course's big issues before you step into the examination hall.   If you are asked "What have been the main causes of urbanisation in the developing world?", you *don't* want to find yourself thinking about this for the first time in the examination hall. You don't really have time. You need to already know what you generally think about this topic, and then be in a position to apply your general understanding to the particular question in the exam.

What you need to do

** So "doing the work" is not enough. You have to take the time to actually understand it **

When you're doing the work during term, it is not enough just to get by. It is not enough just to cover the ground, to have been present in class when the material was covered, to have achieved adequate marks in relevant homework.

Take a little bit of extra time to understand the work as you are doing it. Don't just "get by" on the bare minimum of work. Don't just go through the motions. Take an extra few minutes to work out what you really think about something. Sit back and having a good think about it for yourself. Do you really understand it? Yes, this is "extra" time and will add to the length of time it takes you to finish a piece of work. But this "understanding time" will have a huge impact on your grades at the end of the day.

Understanding something can be tough: Understanding something involves actually applying your brain and thinking about it. But if you want the best results you need to switch your brain to "ON" rather than leaving it in "CRUISE".

What is understanding?

MYTH: People often think of understanding as being some kind of "light bulb" moment of "pure genius", when everything magically becomes clear.

REALITY: Understanding is achieved by asking lots of very simple questions. It is achieved in the process of asking and answering the very simplest questions that you can come up with. There's rarely a "light bulb" moment - understanding is usually achieved gradually.

MYTH: It is sometimes thought that understanding is about holding complicated things in your mind. Understanding is presented as a very complex activity that only complete geniuses could ever possibly hope to participate in.

REALITY: Genuine understanding is the art of making somewhat complicated material as simple as you possibly can. Understanding is all about simplicity. It is about having a cast-iron and extremely clear understanding of the absolute basics. People who really understand something are capable of explaining it really, really simply.

EXAMPLE: One of the questions I have heard asked during the Oxford interview is "how would you explain a credit card to a 5 year old?".

The essence of understanding is simplicity: If you really understand something, you are able to grasp it and explain it in the simplest possible terms.   It is harder to express something slightly complicated in simple language than it is to use fancy words to hide the fact you don't really get it.

Simplicity must come first: Only if you understand something on the simplest level will you be able to understand it on more complex levels, and in more detail. If you understand something on its most simple level, then you can add the detail in later. You should only add the detail once you have a very simple, and therefore very solid, foundation on which to build. You need to work out which way up the Christmas tree goes before you start putting its decorations on!

How to actually understand something

Understanding is the product of your asking a lot of very short and very simple questions, and then making the effort to think about what the answers might be.

What sort of questions do you need to ask? You need to ask questions of the very simplest kind:

- What is really basically going on here?
- Why did it happen?
- Why is it important?
- How does one part of it fit with another? what is its internal logic?
- Why have I been asked to learn about this in particular?

This process is also known as "thinking critically" about the material. It is about approaching the material actively and with your brain switched to "ON".

Activity vs passivity: Contrast the idea of just reading through your notes and hoping that they somehow sink in. This approach is PASSIVE. But understanding is ACTIVE. You have to engage in the activity of asking lots of very simple questions about the material in front of you.

Making connections is another important aspect of understanding. Try to make connections between the material you are studying and:

- other parts of the course
- the themes of the course
- things that you have studied in other subjects
- current events that you have come across in newspapers or magazines

Making connections like this allows you to understand the material in context. Demonstrating awareness of these connections will show the examiner that you have a higher level of understanding of the material. See the discussion on making connections in Chapter 5 "Perfect essays made easy" (p 105)

Some other techniques:

- **Translating into your own words:** My notes often consist of my "translations" of complex ideas in my notes into terms and language that I find easier to understand. This is my way of trying to simplify and so to understand the ideas in front of me.
- **The blank page** and **teaching the material to someone else:** These are great techniques to gain understanding. Have a look at these and other techniques in the next chapter – Chapter 11 "How to learn stuff".

OUTCOME: The outcome of successfully understanding something is that you will be able to express some possibly complicated ideas in your own words. You start by asking simple questions, and then you produce answers in your own words.

Essential points:

✓ Taking the time to genuinely understand the work is the absolute key to doing well at exams.

✓ Understanding the work properly will allow to actually apply what you know to the questions asked by the examiner. It allows you to adapt the material to the specific question the examiner has asked.

✓ Remembering material is much easier if you actually understand it.

✓ The essence of understanding is simplicity. You need to have very solid grasp of the most basic points of the material you're studying.

✓ Understanding is achieved by means of asking a lot of very simple questions, and by making connections between the subject matter and other things you know about.

How to learn stuff

What's this chapter about?

This chapter is about what to do when the exams appear on the horizon, from when they are about three months away.

In reality effective preparation starts right from the very first days of the course. Remember Chapter 1 "Finding out what they want to see" and Chapter 2 "How to never waste a moment's work".

This chapter is about what to learn and when to start learning it. It's about finding out the best methods of getting this stuff into your particular head. Everyone's brain works differently, and this chapter sets out a wide selection of techniques some of which should work for you.

But just learning the material isn't enough. Even understanding the material isn't enough. Only practising applying what you understand will give you the experience and the confidence to get the best result you possibly can.

Key principles of revision

- **Learning: You ABSOLUTELY MUST leave enough time for getting it into your head.** You can have the prettiest notes in the world, but if you haven't spent time learning them properly then they are absolutely useless.

- **Genuine understanding:** If you actually understand the material then you will find it much easier to remember (p 160).

- **Active engagement:** Mix up your learning techniques to force your brain to really think about the material in lots of different ways.

- **Practice using the material:** It doesn't just have to go IN to your head, it also has to come OUT in the exam where you will need to APPLY it to the question. This takes practice (p 184).

Learning time

CLASSIC MISTAKE (1): Spending too much time perfecting your notes

> *Don't get bogged down creating a perfect set of notes, beautifully illustrated using 17 colours of gel pens. Emily*

CLASSIC MISTAKE (2): Not giving enough time to learning the notes that you've made. Many people spend a lot of time making notes, perhaps assuming that while doing this the material is somehow "sinking in". Unfortunately a very nasty surprise is often waiting for them in the exam.

> *I know one really important thing I learned was not to assume I'd taken information in just because I'd read it. Sally*

CLASSIC MISTAKE (3): Pretending to yourself that you know something when you don't. You ABSOLUTELY MUST come to an HONEST and realistic assessment of what it is that you know, and don't know. The only way of making sure that you know your stuff is to TEST YOURSELF TO MAKE SURE THAT YOU ACTUALLY REALLY KNOW IT.

DANGER: Finding out in the exam that you don't actually know the material is a COMPLETE DISASTER. If you kid yourself that you know something when you don't, when the exam comes round you will be completely stuffed.

Repetition is key: You will have to keep coming back to it. Short bursts of learning, repeated over a period of time, is the best way of getting it all into your head.

Allocate time specifically for learning: You need to devote as much time as you can possibly afford to simply learning the material and becoming comfortable with it. You have to budget for and plan specific "learning time" as part of your revision.

How much learning time is required? That depends on the nature of the exam. At Oxford we were examined on over two years of material all at the end of the course. I devoted five weeks specifically to learning just before the exams. No new material, just learning. The point is that we're not talking about a few hours here or there – days or weeks will be required. More generally, you want to give more time to learning rather than less.

What to learn

How many topics to you need to cover? How much of the course do you actually need to prepare for the exam?

Everything? For many exams you simply have to learn everything on the course. You don't know what is going to come up, there is little choice of question within the exam, and so you simply have to cover all the ground.

Or is there a choice? Other exams involve a lot more choice, which means that you have the option of employing a variety of different tactics:

- **"Bin and win":** This may allow you to set some aspects or areas of the course to one side - to "bin and win".
- **DANGER - "bin and lose":** The obvious risk here is that you don't learn enough topics, or that your topics don't come up, and so you get caught out. This is an absolute disaster and must be avoided at all costs.
- **Emergency topics:** In exams where there is a greater degree of choice, it may be worth having an "emergency topic" or two up your sleeve. These are not topics that you actively want to write about, but are ones that you can have something to write if the questions you want don't come up. It is absolutely critical that you are not left stranded without enough topics to write about. Knowing a little about a topic can allow you to scramble some kind of answer, but you won't be able to do this if you know absolutely nothing. (See p 206 on "Scrambling around"!)

Find out what they're looking for: Look at the past papers, and ask your tutor and other students about the best tactics. See generally Chapter 1 "Finding out what they want to see".

Exam choice and your term's work: The level of choice available in the exam makes a big difference the work that you need to do during term. If you are definitely not going to prepare a topic for the exam, and can do extremely well without knowing anything about it, then there is little point in doing too much work for that particular topic during term. Instead you should use the time available to maximise your understanding of subjects that you are actually going to answer on in the exam. This isn't about avoiding work. It's about focussing your efforts on work that will actually pay off when it comes to doing the exam.

Hints: If you get told what's going to be on the exam this can be extremely important.

- **Don't miss any hints!!** Clues are often given in "revision classes". Make sure you're in the front row. Come prepared with a few questions – this is a great time to get personal input from your tutor.

- **Ask for hints:** This is perfectly normal, and the worst your tutor can do is to laugh and say is "no hints". If you don't ask, you don't get.

- **Changing tactics:** If you get told that a certain topic is definitely coming up it can be worth completely changing the subjects you are preparing in the light of this. TIME is the key factor here. Do you have time to change tactics or is it too late?

- **DANGER:** The tip may not be exact. While tutors may be happy to give out a hint or two, they are usually unwilling to give out the precise details of the questions in an exam. So the question in the exam is unlikely to be *exactly* the same as their hint. There will usually be a different angle, or a different twist. So don't go in thinking "this is going to be so easy". It is very likely that you will still have quite a bit of thinking to do in order to apply what you know to the question actually asked.

The depth of learning required

- **Familiarity:** Being able to rhyme the material off isn't enough. Only genuine familiarity will allow you to actually apply what you know to the questions in the exam, under pressure. The emphasis in the exam has to be on THINKING how to APPLY the material to the question, rather than on struggling to REMEMBER what the actual material is in the first place.
- **Detail:** e.g. quotations. Detail allows you to showcase your understanding. Example - you may have a good theoretical understanding of Hamlet's character, but you need quotations to decorate your understanding with relevant factual knowledge.

How much to learn

How much detail do you need to learn? Think carefully about this.

DANGER: There is a real danger of trying to learn too much. Remember, exams are not just about what you know. They are also about applying what you know to the exam questions at hand.

What you are trying to achieve here: In order to be able to apply your knowledge and understanding to the question, the material has to be *manageable*. It needs to be in *building blocks* that you can make use of to answer the question. You need to be able to juggle the material in the time-pressured environment of the exam.

> *Don't go in with a combine harvester when what you really need is a lawnmower. Craig*

Taking notes: Remember, when you are taking your notes in the first place, think about how much detail you will need for the exam. There is no point in taking extremely detailed notes if there is no way you will be able to learn them for the exam!

Quotations: Choose quotations that are multi-purpose. Example - choose a quotation that gives insight into Gatsby's character, but that also gives insight into the broader theme of decay. You can use this quotation in a question on Gatsby, OR in a question on the theme of decay. Flexibility is key. Don't try to learn too many.

Detail: Use detail as evidence to back up more theoretical points. So, for example, if you are saying "Towards the end of 1943 Hitler became more anxious about the situation in the East", then accompany this with "as indicated in Goebbels' diaries of that year".

Structuring your notes: When you're putting your notes together put the most important points first. You may not have time to wheel out everything that you know on a particular topic in the exam. Put your best points first so that if time is tight then you will definitely get these ones down on paper. Learn them in this order.

Your notes should be final: They should contain the information that you will be going into the exam with. You will be spending a lot of time understanding and learning these notes. They should not be added to or changed in any significant way. Keep it simple for your brain. It will be difficult enough to master one set of notes and ideas without having to wrap your head around all sorts of little changes and revisions that you might make.

Which subject to work at

At any given moment, which subject should you be working at?

Keep a list of the work that you need to do over the next few days. Writing it down means that you don't have to try to carry it around in your head the whole time. See "The Power of the List" (p 46).

Work at your weakest subject. My general tactic was to work at the subject I thought was my weakest, until it stopped being my weakest any more.

DANGER: Don't get bogged down. You can't afford to spend too much time on one area or in one subject.

DANGER: Don't neglect your strongest subjects. A friend of mine who got a Double First in history from Cambridge got a "B" in GCSE History and in GCSE English – her two strongest subjects!

Balance one subject off against another:

- Trade off a session on a subject that you enjoy against a session of a subject that you don't particularly enjoy.
- Balance a subject that forces you to think a certain way, with a subject that forces you to think a completely different way e.g. Maths and English Literature. Play them off against each other to keep things fresh.
- Balance harder tasks with easier tasks. e.g. use doing mindless admin as a kind of break from more intellectually demanding tasks.
- But forget balance if you just really want to do some particular subject that day. If you want to do that work, then run with it.

Revision and learning: General points

HOW NOT TO DO IT: The classic mistake to make here is to sit reading through your notes hoping that it is somehow "going in". It isn't! Kidding yourself that it is could mean that you end up having a pretty nasty surprise in the exam.

Everyone's different. Have a go at using each of the methods outlined below, and work out which is best for you. Experiment!

Actually understanding the material in the first place is by far the most effective method of remembering it. If you understand something, it exists in your head whether you like it or not. How do you ride a bike? You don't have to remember this, because you just kind of know it. See Chapter 9 for discussion of how to genuinely understand the work.

Mix it up to beat boredom and to find out which method works best for you.

Doing a little is better than doing nothing at all. You want to avoid days where you mean to work but end up doing little or nothing. Learning is intense so keep your work sessions short (p 30), and have a look at the section on beating procrastination (p 51).

Revision and learning: Specific techniques

Summarising:

This was always my key method of revising. I think it's really useful for the following reasons:

- **Simplicity:** Understanding is all about keeping things simple, and summarising forces you to do this.
- **Active processing:** Summarising forces you to put things into your own words. This means that you are actively processing the material in front of you, rather than just reading it and letting it wash over you.
- **Output:** Summarising gives you a neat set of notes that you can test yourself on to find out how much you really know.

```
I had to take notes of everything as I was
reading it to keep myself focused, even taking
notes of my notes.  Sally
```

Use your summaries to test yourself: Simply take a blank sheet of paper and a pen and try to write out the summary from scratch. Don't cheat by having just looked at the relevant material. The first few times you do this you will probably be shocked and depressed at how little you know. But it's better to find out now rather than in the exam. Repetition is key, and it may take you many efforts to be able to reproduce your summaries accurately. Treat it like a game. Do this as many times as it takes for you to be able to write out your notes from memory. Realistically, this might take anywhere between three and ten repetitions. When you're testing yourself again don't bother writing out stuff in full if you're absolutely certain that you know it – focus your efforts on the material that you struggled with on the previous occasion. Don't worry about making mistakes – this is the process of learning.

> *Write it, write it and write again. Write your formulae down on as many post it notes, scraps of paper and backs of envelopes as possible. You do not need to write them all out beautifully in your best writing, far better to scribble your formulae down, check that you've got them right, bin the scrap of paper and repeat this every day before the exam. This kind of studying takes MINUTES but will reap huge benefits in the exam. Emily*

Summarise your summaries: This forces you to simplify and so to understand the material on the most basic level.

> *Write notes. And then re-write them shorter – like preparing giving a speech - write it out in full and then go back to key words. Craig.*

The Blank Page: Before you even look at your notes on that topic, sit for a few minutes with a blank sheet of paper and jot down your understanding of what the material you're going to study is actually about. The blank page forces you to switch your brain to "ON", and to actively think about what you *really* know about something.

> *The most useful study tool you will ever use is a simple blank sheet of paper. Matt*

Revision cards:

- Buy those small cards slightly smaller than a postcard and use them to write notes on so that you can test yourself.
- *Write one topic per card. You can carry these with you and look at them in the car/ bus trips. Liz*

- Don't write too much on any one card – you could even cut the cards in half if you like. Look at them as "triggers", rather than as your "proper" notes on that topic.
- Use colour, adding pictures, sticking on pictures from magazines etc. Do whatever it takes to make them memorable!
- Take your cards everywhere and study them in random moments e.g. waiting for the bus. Short bursts of time like this are ideal for memorisation.
- Prioritise: Spend more time studying the cards that you are having a difficult time with.

Spidergrams:

What are they? Spidergrams look like spider's webs or like the spokes of a bicycle. For example - if you were doing a spidergram for "causes of the First World War", you could have one spoke for political causes, another for economic causes, another for "arms build-up", and another for nationalism, and so on. Each of the spokes can branch off in further directions, so "political causes" could be divided into "short-term" and "long-term". You can write key facts along or branching off each of the spokes. Google images has lots of good examples.

Why are they useful? Drawing a spidergram forces your brain to turn ideas into a picture, and so it makes your brain think in a different way. and forces you to genuinely engage with the material.

How to do them: Use different colours, draw pictures or cut out pictures and stick them on to help you remember it.

Test yourself by drawing these out again and again.

Creating diagrams: The process of doing this forces you to actively engage with the material. You also have to ask yourself about what's really important and about how different aspects of the material relate to each other. Converting information into visual form means that you have to think about it a different way.

Go up the wall:

> *I remember having lots of quotations, references and things I had to learn written out in bright colours and stuck up around my room, which definitely helped. Sally*

Some successful science students even get a whiteboard for their room - it's nice not to be chained to your desk when you're trying to solve a problem.

Use colour:

> *I used to write out the chunks of my notes in different colours (no colour scheme or anything – I just found that contrasting blocks of colour helped my simple mind to navigate a page). Clarke*

Say it out loud:
Reading your notes out loud forces you to focus on the content of your notes, and is a surprisingly effective way of helping you to remember them. Also, see if you can explain the topic to yourself from scratch – it's a bit like the "Blank Page" test outlined above. Pretend that you are giving a lecture or explaining it to a friend.

Record your work:
Again, it's all about processing the material, and forcing your head to think about it in a different way. Selecting which material to include in your recording forces you to evaluate and engage critically with the issues in front of you. Listen to your recordings as a means of revision. Some people play tapes like this while they are drifting off to sleep.

Mnemonics:
Medical students are particularly famous for making up rhymes like this. They don't really help understanding at all, but may help you to get stuff into your head. For example:

- Richard of York Gave Battle In Vain - Red, Orange, Yellow, Green, Blue, Indigo, Violet.

For GCSE chemistry my friend Helen and I made up a series of songs to describe things we needed to remember – which took us rather a long time (and involved a great deal of giggling and dancing about) – but the effectiveness of which is proven by the fact that 17 years later, I can still describe to you the process of producing iron in the blast furnace, and could probably draw you a diagram, merely by humming to myself the tune of 'Down in the Jungle, Where Nobody Goes'. When the first question on a chemistry paper came up - 'Describe the process of making iron in a blast furnace', I could see Helen's head bobbing up and down as she remembered the song... Helena

Lists: If there are 4 arguments for something, and three against, knowing the number of things you are looking for can help you to remember it. Work out what the key word in each argument is, and then create a mnemonic to help you remember it.

At A Level I quite often made numbered lists to help me... if I knew that I had a list of 'Seven Liberal Achievements' by Gladstone in his first term as prime minister, and another list of 'Five Not So Liberal Things', simply knowing the number of items I should be aiming for would help me remember them all on the day. Helena

Number tricks:

My best friend's telephone number is 224073. Here's how I remember it:

- 22. Two little ducks (bingo).
- 40. My next major birthday, alas.
- 73. One less than my highest ever score at cricket.

The power of the imagination:

EXAMPLE: *"Augustus entwined himself about the body of the state". (Seneca).*

Remember this quotation by building on the vivid image of the snake that is already there: "AuguSSSStuSSS entwined himself about the body of the SSState...", this quotation being by SSSSeneca. Why not draw a picture of a snake at the side of the page in your notes, or as part of your spider diagram?

Get someone to test you: If someone in your family can be persuaded to help you out, then mix it up by getting them to test you on the material. This process will force the material into different parts of your brain, and make you think about it differently, and more simply.

Trying to explain the material to someone else is a great way of helping you to understand it. Being able to answer the very simplest questions about a topic is a sure sign that you actually understand it yourself.

Discussing the material with someone else who knows about it can also be good. To participate in this kind of conversation, you need to make use of the material that is inside your head. This is precisely what you will need to do in the exam.

Form study groups with the expectation that members will teach parts of the subject to the group. Comprehension and memory retention is much better when teaching than passively reading or listening. Kirk

Helping others: Explaining something to someone who is struggling with the material is a great way of clarifying and solidifying it in your own mind. Their questions and misunderstandings will force you to twist and turn that material inside your head in a slightly different way, and in doing so you'll get a better look at it yourself.

Revising with other people:

- o "Study buddies" can really help with motivation:
  - • You are both in it together, and can spur each other on.
  - • You can help each other to understand the material.
  - • Explaining topics to your study partner can help you to understand it more deeply yourself.
- o **MASSIVE DANGER:**   "Revising" with other people all too easily turns into "just chatting" with other people. My view is that if you want to chat, chat. But if you want to revise, then get down to some serious work.
- o **Tips to avoid group work turning into a waste of time:**
  - ▪ Chat at the beginning: Set aside 5 minutes for everyone to talk at the beginning before getting "down to business"
  - ▪ Keep it brief: If you allocate only half an hour for each meeting then there won't be any time for waffle or distraction
  - ▪ Prepare in advance: If everyone prepares something in particular in advance then it's much more likely to be productive.
  - ▪ Get everyone to agree what they are going to prepare for next time.

Get out and about: When you're in the learning phase why not get out for a walk if the weather's good. You won't have too many bits of paper to get blown around, and it's just another context where you might think differently about the material, and remember it just that little bit more.

Cramming: Ideally the last few days of your preparation for the exam will be calm. If you have devoted lots of time to learning the main danger should be boredom rather than panic. However, even if you are well-prepared, don't overlook the possible benefits of revising your notes right up to the moment you walk into the exam. You can literally be reading something one minute and then writing about it ten minutes later. Answer this question first, so that it is still fresh in your head. Get up early and leave yourself an hour before the exam to look over some notes. Just pick one or two topics – don't try to look over everything, or you will just get confused.

Bring the work to life

How can you prevent revision becoming stale? Make use of:

- YouTube clips
- TV / DVD / Video
- Films
- Museum trips
- Google around and see what you can find

How is this useful for the exam? Good question – this is definitely the way you should be thinking! (See Never Waste a Moment's Work – Chapter 2) Yes, strictly speaking you are unlikely to be examined on the YouTube clip that you watch of Thatcher's resignation speech. But it may spark off a more general interest in the subject as a whole, and therefore motivate you to do more work overall.

Squeezing out another session

A 15 minute session can be better than none at all: You can definitely achieve something in 15 minutes, particularly if you're doing high-intensity work such as learning.

A 5 minute session can be better than none at all: Squeeze in a look at your learning cards while you are waiting for the bus. Repetition is key.

Chop and change your location: You don't have to be chained to your desk. Get out and about to different libraries, coffee shops, and your grandparents' house. Mix it up to beat boredom. Studies show that you're actually more likely to remember material if you learn it in lots of different places.

Play off different subjects against each other: When you are tired of revising English Literature, take a break and then do some Maths. Different subjects use different parts of the brain, and doing something completely different may help to keep you interested.

Play off one type of work against another: When you are tired of writing your essay but still feel the need to do something productive why not file that pile of notes away, or take your books back to the library instead?

> *Remember once the exam is over, you won't have to do any more revision on that subject again.*
> *Liz*

Maybe it's just time for a break: If you can't concentrate then it won't be going in properly, so make the most of your time by getting out and relaxing properly, so that you can come back fresh for your next session.

The importance of practice: Past papers

Remember: Exams aren't just about what you know, they're about how well you can apply what you know. Applying your knowledge is a skill that you can get better at with practice. But many only people go through the process of applying their knowledge to questions once a year – in the exam itself! This is crazy!!

> *Past papers are really important in preparing. I use them during revision, usually in the 4-6 weeks before the exam, both to get in the swing of answering but also to highlight any gaps that I may have missed in my revision. Ellie*

How to make use of them:

Look again at the type of questions that are asked: Think carefully about how you would approach each type of question.

Do a paper under exam conditions and ask your tutor if they will mark it.

> *Write practice timed essays and have them marked - there's no substitute for it. No-one writes longhand anymore so few students these days will really be in the habit of handwriting essays - they will need to practise. Sally*

Alternatively just plan each essay rather than writing the whole thing out. Take the same amount of time that you would allocate to planning in the exam (i.e. probably ten minutes or less).

Or simply read through the questions and consider how you might answer them.

Practice struggling: Sometimes your questions don't quite come up and you have to scramble a question at the end of the exam. In this situation your ability to keep fighting and to patch together some kind of reasonable answer could make a big difference to your overall grade. So don't just practice doing juicy questions that you have plenty to say about.

See the section on "Scrambling around" for ideas on how to do this (p 206).

The importance of practice: Mock exams

It's the end result that matters (1): The results of mock exams simply don't matter *except* where predicted grades may be based on your results in the mocks.

Some people argue that mocks are a good opportunity to practice your exam technique. By all means, use them this way and make the most out of them.

However my personal view is that mocks are in fact of only very limited use: It is highly unlikely that you will have learnt the material anywhere near as well as you would have for the real exam, and the adrenaline won't really be pumping either. For these reasons, sitting a mock is not actually that similar at all to doing the real thing.

Never waste work: You should waste as little of your time as possible preparing work that will only be of use for the mock itself. All the notes that you prepare, and all the understanding work that you carry out, must be of direct use for the real exam.

It's the end result that matters (2): It is perfectly possible to crash and burn in the mocks, but to do extremely well in the real thing.

The mocks are not your only opportunity to practice: Earlier years at school will have given you plenty of opportunity to do so. Use exams during these years to practice your technique, to practice doing well, and to practice winning. You can also use past papers in the run-up to the exam.

Practising types of question you have not done before

You may occasionally come across a type of question that you have simply never done before, particularly if you are studying a new subject.

DANGER: There's a danger of messing up this type of question, not because you aren't capable of doing it well, but because you don't know how to do it properly.

Remember the basic principle: You can't give them what they want if you don't know what they want.

How to find out what they want:

- Ask your tutor to explain how to approach these questions. Ask for clarification if you are still not sure. Maybe they will have an example of a piece of work that has been given a very high mark. Make sure you get detailed feedback on your answers to new types of question. Do an extra question of this type and see if your tutor will mark it or go through it with you.
- Ask people in your year and the years above you.
- Examiners' Reports (See Chapter 1).
- Google: If you search for "history source question technique", for example, you will probably come up with some useful material.

How stressed should I be during revision?

MYTH: There's a powerful myth that revision should be "really tough" and that you should be "stressed out" in the run-up to exams. We're all familiar with the stereotype that in order to get any serious work done you need to be slaving away at your desk with match-sticks propping up your eyes.

REALITY: Sure, knowing that the exams are coming up can be stressful. But don't feel that you somehow ought to be more stressed than you actually are. If you've been working hard(ish) and working smart from day one, and have been making the effort to actually understand the material as you've been going along, it will very probably be ok. Keep having as much fun as possible right up to the exams – seeing your friends and having a balanced lifestyle is the best possible way to prevent stress and to keep it all in perspective (See Chapter 9)

Essential points:

- ✓ Start learning early: There's no point in having the prettiest notes in the world if you can't actually remember any of them.
- ✓ The best way of remembering work is to actually understand it in the first place.
- ✓ Test yourself to make sure that you can really remember the material. Prove that you know it.
- ✓ Find out which learning techniques work for you.
- ✓ Practise applying your knowledge to actual questions. For many people the first time they do this is in the exam... crazy!

12

Exam technique

(preparing for success)

What's this chapter about?

I've never met anyone who actually likes exams, and I suspect that you haven't either. What we're trying to do here is to minimise the pain required for you to get the grades you want.

This chapter is about creating the right mindset to do well, and also about getting some practicalities correct so that you have less to worry about. This sections coming up are as follows:

- How to have nerves of steel
- Crazy mistakes to avoid
- Practical details that you have to get right

How to have nerves of steel: Rely on your preparation

This is going to sound harsh, but it's the truth: The best way to avoid nerves before an exam is to have done a load of work in preparation for it. If you know your stuff there really is only so nervous that you are ever going to get.

You'll notice that these chapters on "exam technique" are actually quite short, whereas the chapters on how to prepare for an exam are quite long. If you've prepared properly, there really isn't a huge amount more to say.

Chris Hoy, the Olympic gold medal-winning cyclist, trains on Christmas Day so that he knows no-one will have prepared harder than him. Knowing that you have prepared really, really well, is also a massive psychological boost.

Don't feel that you have to be nervous: People always say, "You must be nervous". Why? If you have prepared well, you will be ready to go in and show the examiner what you've got.

There is nothing magic about doing well at exams: You've done the work. You've done the revision. There's always more in your head than you realise. Now, get in there, THINK before answering the question, and bring home the bacon!

Nerves are good – they show you want it: But what really shows you want it is the ton of work that you have done in preparation. And that work will count double if you have been "working smart".

Everyone Is nervous: Most people will have prepared less well than you. Just imagine how nervous they will be. If you have prepared well, you are definitely going to pass. The only issue for you is whether or not you nail it.

You need the nerves: Quick thinking and quick writing require adrenaline. They require nervous energy. Turn the nerves to your advantage.

Get a good night's sleep the night before: Research shows that lack of sleep is a big factor in not being able to stay calm. Set multiple alarm clocks so that you aren't worried about sleeping in. If you can't sleep then just lie there and rest, chances are you'll drop off.

How to have nerves of steel: Undermining negative thoughts

It's not about being perfect: An exam is an imperfect exercise. The examiners know that you are performing under time pressure, and are not expecting perfection. There are usually lots of different ways of doing well in an exam – it's an art, not a science.

Uncertainty is ok and should not be confused with nerves: Yes, you don't know what's going to be on the exam. But that doesn't mean that you need to be that worried about it. Your preparation and familiarity with the material will mean that you are able to adapt to whatever the examiner throws at you.

The examiners want you to do well: They have no reason to want you to fail. If the examiner is your teacher they will want to be able to give you good marks because it reflects well on their teaching. Give them the opportunity to give you a good mark.

Don't talk to people just before the exam: No matter how well you have prepared, other people will know things that you don't know. Avoid conversations that might make you nervous, lose confidence, or become confused. Be on time for the exam but don't be too early. Have your "business hat" on. You are here to perform well in the exam, not to joke around.

How to have nerves of steel: Keeping your cool

Take a break: If you feel yourself start to panic then take a short break in the middle of the exam. Deep breaths. Set down your pen so that you're not gripping onto anything.

Relaxation techniques such as yoga or breathing exercises may be useful for people who get very nervous. If you are one of these people then you develop these techniques in advance.

Talk to yourself! It might be worth developing something that you can tell yourself during the exam, even if it's just "Keep going!" or "Fight!". Some cricketers, for example, say "watch the ball" to themselves every time the bowler is running in. Little repetitions like this can help keep you in the zone. Another technique is to talk rationally to yourself e.g. "Very few people actually fail, and I have done a lot of work so there's no reason that I shouldn't do just fine".

How to have nerves of steel: Visualisation

What?? Imagining your success can help you achieve it in real life. If you have spent a lot of time thinking positive thoughts about your going into an exam and doing really well, then you are more likely to perform strongly on the day.

Do people really do this? Yes indeed – this technique is used a lot in the world of sport. Buy any book on sports psychology and visualisation will be discussed at length. Have you noticed that athletes often have that distant look in their eyes just before a race? They're pre-living their own success.

Here's how to visualise your success

Imagine what's going to happen in as much detail and as vividly as possible: Imagine the sights, sounds, smells of the examination hall. You're feeling calm, turning over the paper, and you start to plan your answers confidently and effectively. Imagine writing each answer, with more ideas coming into your mind through the power of your subconscious. You imagine yourself weaving this material together and producing a really strong response to the question. All your preparation is paying off.

Imagine all possible scenarios, including versions where the exam is difficult but you respond well to this.

Imagine the experience of actually doing it: You're not just looking on as "part of the audience". Try to live the activity of actually doing it. Then when it comes to the real exam it will almost be something that you have done before.

Repetition is key: If you're going to use this technique then do it regularly at a certain time of day. Alternatively you can just do it whenever you feel like it, whenever it occurs to you, or as one way of combating worries if they should arrive.

Make use of visualisation on the day of the exam: Refresh your imagined experience of success the night before and the morning of the exam.

Use your own memories: Think about exams that have gone well in the past. Remember them as vividly as possible. Allow your vivid memories of past success to merge with your anticipation of future success. You can draw confidence from your past performances. You are good at exams. You've done it before and you can do it again!

Crazy mistakes to avoid

Exams make people behave in funny ways: Under pressure the risk of your making some kind of silly mistake really shoots up. I know clever people who got caught out because they didn't take the simple steps outlined below:

Turn up on the right day! It's a really good start. Get a calendar and use it.

Be clear which subject you are actually being examined on! You'd be surprised how many people mess this one up.

Read the exam paper to the very end: Exams are a lot tougher if you only find the questions you could have answered with two minutes to go. Oooops!

Read the instructions carefully: If they say "2 questions from section A and 2 from section B", then it's a good idea to actually follow this. It can be slightly stressful afterwards if you realise you've messed up. I've seen this first hand, and it isn't a pretty sight.

> *Read the questions properly - I once answered every single question on a GCSE mock history paper, when you only had to do three. Helena*

> *Check what's expected of you - how many questions do you need to answer? Are all the questions compulsory? Even seasoned exam passers have been known to make a basic error in their enthusiasm to get on with the exam! Ellie*

Read the question very carefully: Spending an hour of an A level discussing something that the examiner was not in fact asking about is a very effective way of dropping a grade.

Write quickly but legibly:

- **Speed:** One of my friends can only write 2 and a half pages in an hour. Exams are more about quality than quantity, but this will have cost him marks for sure.
- **Readability:** If the examiner can't read it, they can't give you marks. Don't use biro. Space out your words nicely as this makes your answer easier to read.

Practical details that you have to get right

Location of exam hall: Have a reconnaissance mission at some point before the exam. This will also help you to visualise the scene. Check the day before to make sure there hasn't been a last-minute change.

Fundamentals: Time, date, place, subject, seat number. People frequently mess these up. Aim to arrive at the exam hall five minutes before the exam starts, but make sure you're not late. Find somewhere nearby you can wait away from the crowd. Take your time finding your seat and ask the invigilator for help if necessary.

Student number / identification: Set these by the door the night before so that you can't miss them.

Go to the bathroom: You don't have 5 minutes to waste in the exam.

Eat breakfast before you go in and take a muesli bar or something in with you if you can. All that concentrating is exhausting and you'll need the energy. Sally

Classical music: Has been shown to raise people's IQ temporarily, but significantly, so listen to some on the morning of the exam. Alternatively listen to the music that accompanied your studying that particular topic, to get you back in the zone.

Food / drink: Bring some into the exam. Chocolate increases blood flow to the brain. Bring in a caffeine drink as well to keep you pepped up.

Open up your supplies so that they are accessible before the exam begins. Break up your chocolate in advance. Some people find that chewing gum helps to distract them from exam nerves.

Pens etc: You will also need a pencil and eraser for planning.

Watch or clock: Bring your own in case you're behind a pillar etc.

Filling in your details: Do this before the exam starts so you don't have to worry about it at the end. Do it calmly, and keep it neat to create the right impression.

> *It would be a shame to get all the answers right but then score no marks because you have not put your candidate number on the paper correctly! Ellie*

Paper: Crease the answer booklet's pages before the exam begins, to make it sit more comfortably. Where are you going to jot your planning notes?

Get yourself comfortable: Loosen your top button. Take your sweater off. Make sure the table doesn't wobble. Set your drink and chocolate on the floor beside you. Make that little patch of examination hall your own.

Sickness: If you are sick get a doctor's note and / or tell the examiner (who may be able to take a note of it and attach it to your exam). Go and see the doctor after the exam if necessary.

Essential points:

✓ Everyone's nervous: Nerves show you want to get the result you deserve. If you've prepared well then the exam is almost always ok.

✓ Undermine negative thoughts: The examiner doesn't expect perfection. There are different ways of doing really well. Don't talk to people before the exam.

✓ Harness the power of your imagination: Visualise yourself performing well.

✓ Get the practicalities right: A surprising number of people turn up on the wrong day etc

13

Exam success

(giving them what they want)

What's this chapter about?

This chapter is about how to make your preparation count by doing yourself justice on the day. It's about the nitty-gritty of exam technique.

This chapter's contents are as follows:

- ➤   Choosing your questions
- ➤   The importance of planning
- ➤   Writing your answers
- ➤   Getting your timing right
- ➤   How to scramble an answer that you don't know much about

Choosing your questions

Have a plan for how you are going to approach for the beginning of the exam. This will help keep you methodical and focussed.

Write down anything you are worried about remembering at the very beginning. (e.g. dates, formulas, facts etc).

Don't rush: Staying cool at the beginning will set the tone for how you approach the whole of the exam. Stay in control. Deep breaths. Focus.

Choosing your questions: Read through all the questions at the beginning of the exam so that your subconscious can start working on them straight away.

> *Decide which questions you will answer before you begin. I imagine a little man running round the brain opening doors for the information it will need later, even as you begin the first answer...it's worth getting him going from the start! Helena*

Reading through will also hopefully reassure you that this exam is not in fact impossible and so will help you to keep your nerves at bay.

Which question to begin with?

You don't have to do the questions in the order that they come up in the exam paper. You could:

o   Start with your best question, so that you gain confidence.
o   (Alternatively) Start with a question that you can do quite well, but not your best question, so you can get "warmed up" before doing your best one.
o   If you have just been reading about a particular topic before going into the exam, and then it comes up, then you should answer this question first.
o   Save the hardest problem question to last. Get the easy marks in the bag, then tackle the more difficult stuff. This reduces the risk of getting stuck and so not having the time to do questions that you might have completed fairly easily.

Choosing the more difficult option: If you want to get the highest marks then choose the more challenging questions, because these will give the better students more of a chance to shine. The more difficult a question is, the more important it is to attack the question, and to give more time to planning your answer.

Planning – THINK!!

** Planning is absolutely the most important part of any exam **

Remember: Exams are not just about **WHAT** you know. The best students will show their ability by **APPLYING** what they know to the questions at hand.

CLASSIC MISTAKE: The danger here is that you see a word or phrase that you recognise, and that you then vomit out everything you know about that topic. This is a great way to get a B or C.

Planning is the same as THINKING: Switch brain to "ON" and take a few minutes to actually think. In the time pressure of the exam, this is actually quite difficult to do. It's much easier to just vomit out something vaguely relevant. The fact you are covering paper with writing is extremely tempting because it allows you to pretend to yourself that you are actually achieving something, even if you are charging off towards a grade much lower than the one you are really capable of.

What you need to do: Before picking up the ball, make sure that you are going to be running in the right direction!

This is where understanding the work pays off: You will only be able to *apply* the material to the question at hand if you are sufficiently familiar with it and actually really understand what's going on.

You will ALWAYS need to plan: You may have prepared an essay plan on a particular subject. But the question that the examiner asks will never be exactly the same as the question that you have prepared. There will always be *some* difference, and there will usually be *quite a big* difference. The key thing is to adapt the material you've learnt and use it to answer the question that the examiner has actually asked.

Thinking takes TIME: So give it the time it requires. Many people are so obsessed with starting to write that they don't take the time to plan properly. You need to spend time in the exam actually thinking about what you are going to write. The time you spend staring into space, or jotting down a few notes, is the real moment when the exam is either won or lost.

Imagine you are someone else reading the question: How would your teacher or university Professor answer it? What would they pick up on? This little trick may help give you a little distance from the question, space that you can use to THINK a little. (I have also come across this technique in the world of sport e.g. golfers imagining that Rory McIllroy is accompanying them on their round, giving them advice).

Practicalities of planning

- Use a pencil so that you can make changes more easily.
- Use keywords rather than writing out full sentences.
- Space your plan out nicely so that you can add things in.
- Plan all your essays at the beginning of the exam.
- Plan your planning: know in advance how long you are going to spend on it so that you don't give it too long.

Writing your answers

Before you write your answer: Have a quick look at your plan again. Listen to your subconscious: has your brain come up with any further angles or information? Quite often the best answer takes time to emerge. Listen to that little voice, listen to that nagging doubt.

Just say it: Remember the general principles of writing (p 107). Keep it simple, spit it out.

Don't try to write everything you know: Apply what you know to the question at hand. You probably won't have time to write every single point from your notes on that topic. Master the art of writing only what's relevant.

Leave a gap at the end of each answer so that you can add more stuff in easily if it occurs to you later. The examiner doesn't really care about how much paper you use.

Timing

> *Sticking to the time is so important – it's such an easy thing to get wrong and it can make a huge difference if you misjudge it. Matt*

Do not mess this up: You absolutely, absolutely have to get the timing of your exam right. If you don't, then your prospects of getting the grade you want will be in massive, massive trouble. No matter how good your previous answers, you will basically be stuffed. You MUST be extremely strict with yourself in the exam to stick with the timings that you have worked out beforehand.

DANGER: It's amazing how some otherwise extremely smart people can really get it completely wrong on this point. One of the smartest guys I know from Oxford dropped a grade because of this. I remember asking his best friend,

> *"So, I suppose Rick got his First?"*
>
> *"Well, he would have if he had finished any of his papers"*

How long to plan for: If you have an hour to write an essay, I would suggest planning for at 10 minutes, or possibly slightly longer. You will still have plenty of time to write, but it's the quality of your ideas that is important. If you have forty-five minutes to write an essay I would suggest planning for 6-7 minutes.

Have your timings worked out in advance: Before the exam work out how long you are going to give to planning, and how long to writing.

> ***Example:*** *So, if it's a three hour exam with three essays, and you are going to give ten minutes planning to each, and the exam begins at 9 am, then you will start writing your first essay at 9.30, your second at 10.20 and your third at 11.10.*

How things can go very wrong: In the above example if you run over time by just ten minutes in each of your first two essays, then you have only thirty minutes to write your third, which is not going to be enough.

Aim to finish two minutes before the end: If you finish exactly when the examiner says "pens down" then you have misjudged it - you might just as easily have been going to finish a few minutes after the end, in which case you might not have got half of your last conclusion written. Conclusions are one of the most important parts of an essay, and so this could be pretty damaging to your mark.

Salvage operations: If you have messed up the timing, then switch to bullet points. You must complete the questions in some shape or form. Write "TIMING" at the end, and hope that the examiner is in a good mood.

If you have a minute or two at the end:

- Check the answers you have marked as ones to go back to if you have time.
- Read through your answers: There may be some details that you have forgotten to include under the time pressure of the exam.
- Tidy up your writing: An examiner in a bad mood might simply not make the effort to decipher your hand-writing.

The mid-exam break

Crazy as it sounds it can actually be a good tactic to take a very short break in the middle of an exam.

How long should this break be? Very short - maybe between 15 seconds and a minute.

Why is this a good tactic?

- Normal concentration span is about 40 minutes, according to psychologists.
- A break will give your brain a chance to relax, refresh, and to get ready to move onto the next topic.
- New ideas might occur to you while you are relaxing

What to do during your break: Stick your hand up and get some more paper. Eat some chocolate.

A few more quick tips

Abbreviations: If you have to write a long word, like "Thucydides", then the first time you write it put (T) just after, and use this abbreviation from that point onwards.

If this saves you writing out Thucydides 20 times, then it might have gained you the time to write an extra paragraph.

Adding bits in: If you forget to include a point and want to add it in at the end or at the bottom of the page then just put a big star beside where you should have included it, and another big star beside where you have written it. The examiner will not be bothered by this.

Space your work out so that you can add further material in if necessary. Leave about six lines before starting a new question.

Open book exams: You never have enough time to actually look much up, so learn the material by heart in just the same way that you would do for an ordinary exam.

Scrambling around

This section applies mainly to essay-based subjects. It relates to that awkward situation where you have to answer a question but don't actually know that much at all about how to do so ☺

Here is what to do when you find yourself having to answer a question when you are innocent of knowledge:

- **Cramming:**

   People say you should take it easy and stop reading notes and revising desperately just before the exam, which is good advice if you've done lots of work and you know your stuff already. For people who haven't done any or enough work, however, cramming is a great idea. One hour in the morning before an exam can be enough to learn a few basic pieces of information or quotations or theories and this can take you all the way from not being able to answer any questions, to being able to pretend you know what you're talking about and

> *have a basic stab at several. That's what I*
> *reckon. But then it's probably wiser to do a*
> *bit more work than I ever did in the first*
> *place. Albertine*

Knowing very, very little is much, much better than knowing absolutely nothing at all. Knowing very little means that at least you have *something* to work with.

- **Planning:** Planning your answer is even more important than normal in this situation. Given that you are "information light", it's vital that you make best use out of the few shreds of information that you do actually possess.

- **Drawing on what you know:** You may know more than you think. Try to uncover aspects of the question that you do actually know about (but make sure that you take the time to explain or argue how what you are saying is in fact relevant). What were the broader themes of the course? Try to tie what you know in with any broader themes that you are aware of.

- **Attacking the question:** The question gives you something to work with, and so engaging with the specific terms that the examiner used is key. You will get credit for engaging with the question, and may give a reasonable impression that you are attempting to answer it even if you don't have a huge amount of information with which to back this up. You can actually raise quite a lot of intelligent questions about a topic, even if you don't happen to know the answers to them (See p 90).

- **Drawing on other areas of knowledge:** See if you can make connections between this subject and other issues that you do actually know about. So, for example, you may not know much about 1920s politics, but if you once studied a work of literature from that period you might be able to relate it to the question and so get a paragraph out of that. This would certainly be better than writing nothing at all – you might even get credit for using an "interdisciplinary" approach.

- **Get theoretical:** You may not know many of the facts, but you might have an idea about some relevant theories. In the Baldwin example, if you know something about Marxism, then outline this and apply it to Baldwin. What might British Marxists have made of Baldwin? The key point here is that you are actually applying your theoretical knowledge to the question at hand.

Fight!

Fight your very hardest in the exam.

** You must never, ever, ever give up **

If you are finding it difficult - or a particular question difficult - then everyone else will be too, guaranteed.

All you can do is throw the kitchen sink at the exam. People say "all you can do is your best". Well, that's literally true. Just make sure you take the time to THINK so that you will be throwing that sink in the right direction!

The really tough exam: once in a while you will get a nasty surprise - an exam that really knocks you sideways. The important thing here is to **take your time and THINK**. Your genuine understanding of the material will allow you to apply what you know to the questions being asked. Planning is even more important than usual in this situation. Attacking the question (p 90) can give you something to say even if you are somewhat "knowledge light"!

> In one of my final exams I just didn't think that there were any questions I could answer. I remember sitting there literally pulling my hair out at the time. I thought that I had nothing to write, but I kept fighting and managed to scrape something together. After the exams were marked the examiner was

criticised for setting a paper that was too hard, and everyone's marks were bumped up. I ended up with a reasonable mark, which I wouldn't have got if I had just walked out. Alex

Leaving early? Obviously the idea of ever leaving an exam early would be complete lunacy.

Essential points:

- ✓ Take your time.
- ✓ Planning is key: It's so tempting just to start writing. Be strong. You have to take the time to adapt what you know to the question. THINK. Listen to the little voice of your subconscious.
- ✓ Writing: Just spit it out. This isn't a poetry competition!
- ✓ Timing: You simply MUST get the timing right. Know what you are going to do and stick to it.
- ✓ If you have to scramble an answer then give extra time to planning and attack the question to give yourself something to say.
- ✓ Fight! You must never ever, ever, ever give up.

14

After the exam

(you've done it!)

Let me be the first to congratulate you

There are few better feelings than walking out of that examination hall with absolutely nothing to do. You've done it!

This chapter contains some ideas on:

- How to make the most of your time after the exams
- How to make the most of the time off, and,
- Thoughts on the significance of exams more generally

Immediately after the exam

Never discuss an exam immediately afterwards: What's done is done. There will always be things that you could have done differently, even if you have performed very well indeed. The same question can often be answered in very different ways by students who will both be awarded high marks. People often think that they have failed when this is nowhere near being the case.

Relaxation

- **Celebrate in style:** If you have worked hard for the exams, make sure you play hard afterwards.

- **Relax properly:** Spend some days just completely "vegging out". Savour the freedom of having absolutely nothing to do.

- **Make the most of your time off:** You need to be hungry when you come back. Get away on holiday if you can, and see some different stuff. Plan your holiday time so that you make the most of it.

Reviewing your performance

The importance of review: Don't make the same mistakes year after year. Even if you have done very well, it's likely that you could have done better in some significant respects. Step back and evaluate your terms work and revision as a whole. Did you leave enough time for learning? Did you start to become overly tired during the exams?

Get feedback if it is available: Seek out feedback – be proactive. Often it's available, but students don't take it up. Even if you have done well – there may be more room for improvement than you realise. Let your tutor know that you want to see them to get feedback so that they have the chance to have a look at how you - specifically - did in the exam. If they say that your performance was "pretty good" (i.e. if they give you a comment that is so general that it doesn't really tell you very much of use) then push them for specifics on how you can do better next time.

Re-marks: If you think that your performance deserved a better mark, it may well be worth getting your paper looked at again. You may get a more generous examiner this time round.

Picking courses for next year

- **Pick subjects that you are interested in:** You will be more motivated to study these, obviously.
- **Who's teaching that class?** Some tutors get much better results than others. Some tutors are simply unwilling to give high marks. You want a tutor who is capable of imposing some discipline if necessary.
- **Ask people in the year above for their thoughts:** If they say that a particular course involves loads of work and that it's marked very hard then steer clear.
- **Find out how the courses are assessed:** Again, this can vary widely, from 100% coursework to 100% exam. Which do you prefer?
- **New courses can be tricky:** Students don't have past papers to make use of, examiners haven't worked out what they want, tutors haven't perfected their teaching.

Getting ahead

Get ahead for next year - School and university holidays are really quite long, so make the most of this opportunity:

- **Get an overview by reading some basic material:** Use Google or Amazon to find something useful. Wikipedia or even children's books can be good e.g. if you are studying history get hold of the "Horrible Histories" books.

- **Select your books for next term:** Get the reading list in advance, and select which books you think will be most useful for the year's work to come. Then start to have a read at them e.g. if you are doing English Literature then read the books at your own pace "for fun" before you begin to study them properly next year.

- **Maybe even start to get on with the work:**

  At Oxford I did all of my work during the holidays and then mainly just relaxed during term. The way I saw it was that there were a lot more ways to have fun at university than there were when I was stuck at home with my Mum and Dad. So I did the bulk of the work during the holidays at home, and a bit before each tutorial just to refresh my memory. However I spent most of the time during term just having fun, which was brilliant. And I got a First! Sid

  The more work you get done during the holidays, the more free time you will have off later on.

There is more to life than exams

Exam success gives you options: Good exam results open doors. They can help you to get to the university that you want to go to, and to end up doing the job that you want. You can only be a doctor, for example, if you have passed a lot of exams.

But they're not the "be all and end all": No matter what job you do, you'll find that other aspects of life are just as important, if not more important. These include:

- The general ability to get on with people
- Good communication skills
- Taking the initiative
- Being organised
- Willingness to work hard

You might learn these skills on the rugby pitch or playing in a band with your friends. Exams can be important, but they're by no means the whole story.

Some of the very richest people in Britain have famously not passed too many exams at all. Richard Branson, for example, has achieved enormous success after leaving school with one O-Level. To think that exams define success or failure is simply a mistake.

Interestingly, it is also worth noting that "playing the game" turns out to have some rather major similarities with "doing the work properly in the first place". The approach outlined in this book is lean and targeted, but you couldn't really call it unconventional.

If you have found this book anywhere near as useful as I have tried to make it, then do take the time to give it a positive review on Amazon.

Work hard, work smart, have fun, and good luck!

Patrick McMurray

Useful stuff at the back

What's coming up

The contents of this section are strictly optional, rather than essential. But they might come in useful. The sections are as follows:

> - Common spelling mistakes
> - Confusions to avoid
> - Some grammar points
> - Useful words to know
> - Useful Latin words to know
> - Oxbridge applications

Common spelling mistakes

Create the right impression by spelling the following words correctly. Note that all the spellings in this and the following sections are in UK English.

a lot – it's two separate words.	judgement
accommodation	library
address	licence
aggressive	maintenance
consensus	millennium
definitely (NOT definately!)	parliament
environment.	privilege
experience	racist (NOT rascist!)
fascist (don't forget the C!)	restaurant
February	separate (NOT sepERate!)
fulfilment	vacuum
independent (NOT independant!)	

Confusions to avoid

principle vs **principal**

The principal reason that your school's Principal is in charge of the school today, is because she has a sound grasp of educational principles.   She always acts on principle.

stationary vs **stationery**

The car is stationary.

Don't forget to buy lots of stationery.

"Stationary stationery" = Pencils, erasers, pencil sharpeners sitting motionless on a desk.

quotation vs **quote**

"**Quotations**" is the noun, "**to quote**" is the verb.   A "quote" is not English. There is no such thing as a "quote"! It's always "a quotation".

Where and **were**.

They were where they were. (Where deals with location).

If you get this wrong, the examiner will assume that you are not a strong candidate.

There and **their**.

There are their cousins.

Affect and effect.

"Affect" is a verb: "Your ability to communicate clearly will affect your chances of getting this job."

"Effect" is a noun: "The effect of a parent's behavior on a child's future is well documented."

Compliment / complement

"Nice hat!" is a compliment.

"The hat complemented the rest of her outfit".

Criteria and **criterion**

Criteria is plural. The criteria for allowing entry. The singular form of this word is "criterion". e.g. "The sole criterion of admission was that you had to know the national anthem".

Ensure and **insure**.

To ensure something means to act so that it definitely happens, to guarantee that it happens.

You insure a car. It's car Insurance rather than car ENsurance.

Practice and **practise**

Practice is the noun, practise is the verb. I go to my piano practice. I practise the piano. Remember it this way: ICE is a noun.

Literally

This word is frequently misused, a classic example being:

"She was so angry that she literally exploded!"

She didn't. The idea that she exploded is metaphorical rather than literal.

Some grammar points

Getting your grammar right creates a positive impression.   If you make grammatical mistakes then little alarm bells will start going off in the examiner's head.

Some people become obsessed by grammar. I am not one of them.   In reality languages are in constant evolution, and they all change a lot over time.

Use of the apostrophe

There is no apostrophe in the simple plural.

CLASSIC MISTAKE: "Pizza's for sale". Should be: "Pizzas for sale".

Use the apostrophe when something belongs to someone else, otherwise the examiner's head will explode.

Maybe even several examiners' heads will explode. Notice here that if we are talking about things that belong to more than one person, then the apostrophe goes after the "s".

Your and you're

You're wearing your new shoes.

It's and its

The monkey is in its cage. It's playing with its friend, the chimpanzee.

"It's" - *with* the apostrophe - is an abbreviation of "it is".

"Its" - *without* the apostrophe - is the possessive form. i.e. we are talking about something belonging to someone else.

Memory: notice that there is no apostrophe in words like "hers" or "his".

Less and fewer

If you are talking about things that you can actually count – e.g. penguins, polar bears - then use "fewer" and "more".

If the thing you're talking about is indivisible – like ice, sand, air, etc – then use "less" and "more".

The less ice there is, the fewer penguins there will be.

Use of commas

Use commas to indicate where the reader will have to pause a little if he or she wants to be able to understand the sentence.

There are no hard and fast rules here that I am aware of, and my knowledge of commas has been adequate so far.

Quite often, if you want to use commas properly, you will have to use two commas rather than one.

As you can see in the sentence I have just written, the commas almost act as brackets around sub-clause in the middle. The sentence "Quite often you will have to use two commas rather than one" works just fine. But notice that the "if you want to use commas properly" bit doesn't make any sense standing on its own. It's not a proper sentence, and can only work as part of another sentence which it fits into. It is a sub-clause. So here the pair of commas is being used rather like you might use a pair of brackets.

Split infinitives

Some people really get their knickers in a twist about these.

What's an infinitive anyway? An infinitive is the part of the verb meaning "to do something". So, in French, the infinitive of the verb "jouer" (to play) is "jouer" - to play! *To* play.

The basic idea here is that you are not supposed to split the "to" from the other part of the verb i.e. to play. To go. You have to keep the "to" and the other bit together.

So, "to boldly go where no man has gone before" is a grammatical mistake, because it splits the infinitive "to go" with the adverb "boldly". The phrase should be "to go boldly where no man has gone before".

Frankly I don't think split infinitives are really that important. It is perfectly possible never to pay much attention to them, and still to do very well.

Colons and semi-colons

Colons

This is a colon :

A colon is basically saying "this is what's COMING UP, let me tell you about it NOW".

EXAMPLE "The reason I have dwelt on this point is this: without having considered the political context of X, we cannot adequately grasp the significance of events Y and Z".

The colon is basically saying "(1) let me set this point up, (2) here it is".

There is very little agreement on the question as to whether you need to have a capital letter after a colon or not. Just do what seems right at the time. Try to use it consistently i.e. whichever you choose, keep doing it the same way.

Colons can make your writing style more lively.

Semi-colons

This is a semi-colon ;

Think of a semi-colon as being somewhere in between a comma and a full-stop. It indicates that the reader should pause but that that something more on the *same* subject is coming.   It implies a close connection between the first part of the sentence and the second, suggesting that the second part of the sentence contains a fuller development or explanation of the first part of the sentence.

EXAMPLE: By 1943 Hitler's difficulties were certainly mounting up; the Russians were putting pressure on him on the East; the Americans were closing in on the West; and there were a number of pressing internal problems within the Third Reich itself.

Notice how semi-colons can be used in a series.   They are a bit like commas, but the difference is that the idea following each of the semi-colons is flowing from and sprouting off the concept introduced in the very first phrase.

So, the semi-colon is basically saying "(1) X, then (2) Xa, Xb, Xc".

Or, to put it another way:

- X
    - a
    - b
    - c

Both colons and semi-colons can add a touch of class if you manage to use them appropriately.

Useful words to know

Simplicity of expression is key, but sometimes the correct use of a sophisticated word can allow you to express what you think more clearly. If used properly, the words discussed in this section may contribute to your essay making a positive impression. Consult a dictionary if you require more detailed understanding than is provided by the brief definitions and examples offered below.

I have used the British English spellings for all the material in these appendices.

aberration. An exceptional event. The result in the 1914 election was an aberration. It went against the general trend.

adumbrate. To foreshadow. Gatsby's death in the swimming pool was adumbrated by his appearance at Daisy's door, dripping wet.   Noun - adumbration. Verb - to adumbrate.

advocate. To argue for. Labour politicians have recently advocated that we switch to the Alternative Vote electoral system.

ambivalent. To feel more than one thing about a certain issue, these feelings being mutually contradictory. Can also mean "non-committal". "When asked whether she wanted to marry Harry, Sally seemed ambivalent".

ancillary. Subordinate. An ancillary argument is a minor point that contributes to the larger issue. Ancilla is the Latin word for "slave-girl". "The function Y is merely ancillary to the primary function of X".

antithesis. The opposite of. Fascism is the antithesis of liberal democracy. A "thesis" is an argument, or proposition. Its antithesis is the opposite position.

appropriate. We all know what this means, but I mention it because it is a particularly useful word. It can be used to gesture towards a shared understanding between you and the person you are in dialogue with. "We need to deal with this appropriately", means that we need to deal with it according to the procedures and the values that we are both well aware of. I have found it to be a particularly useful word in interviews.

apposite. Means "appropriate" especially when talking about words. That word was particularly apposite, given that...XYZ.

archetype. "He's the archetypal Scot". Means "classic" or even "stereotypical".

stereotype. Stereotypes are general labels that are applied to certain groups of people, these labels being, in many cases, inaccurate. So, Germans are stereotyped as being overly organised. The Irish are stereotyped as being big drinkers and always keen to have some "craic".

assertion. An assertion is a statement that is made without being backed up with any evidence. It is merely asserted, rather than proven. Note also that the word evidence can be used as a verb – "This statement can be evidenced by the point that x.....".

conditioned by. "Conditioned by" basically means that you have to read / understand / consider X in the light of Y. Major arguments can be "conditioned by" context or minor arguments. Our understanding of X can only be reached in the light of certain other factors, which shape our understanding of it. Our discussion of X is conditioned by our earlier discussion of Y.

informed by. Our argument here is informed by our earlier consideration of points a, b and c. This is very similar to "conditioned by".

conjecture. Means "speculation". It will be **unsubstantiated** i.e. there will be no evidence for it.

construe. Means "to interpret as meaning". The legal provision can be construed as meaning x,y,z.

consensus. General agreement.

contested. This means "not accepted by all". If something is contested then there is no consensus on this issue. The legal argument was contested by the other side. "This proposition is contested by Professor T" – this proposition is disagreed with and attacked by Professor T. We will contest this proposition. We will attack and argue against this proposition.

proposition. Means "assertion". An unevidenced statement.

crux. Means the absolute **nub** of the matter. The centre of it. The crux of the argument. "The crux of the issue is that ...".

cumulative. Means "taken together". Cumulatively, these arguments suggest that XYZ.

deductive. This refers to logical deduction. If all boys like apples, and Alex is a boy, then Alex likes apples. Deductive reasoning cannot be argued with, but the truth of its conclusion depends to on the soundness of each of the propositions that construct the argument. So if it's not true to say that all boys like apples, or if Alex is not in fact a boy, then Alex does not necessarily like apples.

Contrast **inductive** reasoning, which is based on what we have observed to be the case so far. Every boy I have met so far likes apples, therefore all boys like apples. Clearly this is limited, in that you can always subsequently meet a boy who doesn't like apples.

to defend the proposition that. In other words: we will argue that XYZ. We will argue in support of the statement that XYZ.

definitive. Total or complete. Smith's latest book is said to be the definitive work on the subject i.e. it is thought to be the "last word" on the subject. It is so **comprehensive** that there is nothing more left to say.

dichotomy. Two diverging strands. Two paths that are heading in different directions. A distinction between X and Y. One can draw a dichotomy between X line of thought, and Y line of thought.

disparate. Different kinds of. Blair's supporters were behind him for disparate reasons. i.e. there were lots of different motivations.

eclectic. To have an eclectic taste in music is to like all sorts of different things, from dance music to opera. Another way of putting this is "**catholic**" i.e. your taste is universal. The Catholic Church considers itself to be the universal church.

empirical. Means grounded in evidence, or grounded in scientific experiment. Is there any empirical basis for that statement, or is it merely an assertion?

eponymous. Named after someone. So, in medicine "Cushing's syndrome" is named eponymously, after the doctor who discovered it.

exemplify. To serve as an example of. That particular MP's speech exemplifies a fairly common position on this issue.

exposition. The setting-out of an argument. His exposition of the argument in favour of renewable energy was entirely convincing.

extraneous. The judge made her decision on the merits of the case, ignoring any extraneous considerations. She did not take any irrelevant matters into consideration.

finite. Limited. Saudi Arabia's oil reserves are considerable, but finite. The opposite of "infinite".

generic. General. The opposite of specific. In medicine a generic drug is one that is mass-produced but that is not sold under a particular brand-name. It is just sold as the drug itself.

hypothesis. A hypothesis is a theory that has not been proved yet with evidence. You construct a hypothesis about what might be the case, and then see if there is evidence to back your theory up. This term is frequently used in science, but is also very widely used elsewhere. Plural = hypotheses.

hypothetical. Pertaining to a hypothesis.

Pertaining to a hypothesis means "relating to a hypothesis".

incremental. Little by little. It happens incrementally i.e. by increments. This is a very useful concept to be familiar with. The development of English common law is, in its very nature, incremental – it has developed **piecemeal**, bit by bit.

inexorable. Inevitable. Seemingly unavoidable. After a certain point, this event was always going to happen. The inexorable rise of China as a world economic power.

inference. To believe something to be the case after having considered the other components of an argument or evidence. "To infer" is not the same as "to assume" – "to infer" is more considered, and is on the basis of having thought about the evidence. It's similar to the idea of "reading between the lines".

inherent. Contained within something and essential to it. His inherent volatility. His inherent frailty. The idea that something is part of a person or idea's character. Part and parcel of it. This word is very similar to **"intrinsic"**.

integral. An essential component of. A vital part of. Davis was an integral part of their team. Important, rather than **supplementary**, or **ancillary**.

irrevocable. Something that cannot be undone.

multi-pronged. Pretty obvious what this means, but it's a useful phrase. You can also refer to the different "prongs" of an argument. **Polyvalent** is quite similar, but means "multi-layered" rather than "multi-pronged".

narrative. Refers to a story. Often used to in relation to a story that someone is making an effort to tell. So, for example, politicians might **construct** a narrative about themselves, by means of emphasising certain points about their past, or certain aspects of their character. This might appeal to voters by giving more of a "story" to their lives, rather than their simply being random individuals who support certain policies. **Narrative history** is chronological rather than analytic or thematic.

constructed. This is an important concept. The key idea here is that there has been a deliberate selection or choice as to how something is presented, and as such how its reality is created. Identity is often said to be constructed in that we choose what to reveal about ourselves to other people, and also in that we construct identities for other people by choosing which aspects of their character to emphasise.

nuanced. Subtle. A nuanced analysis is one that appreciates the complexities of what it's discussing. It shows a willingness to appreciate that more than one factor was at play. The opposite of a nuanced analysis would be something like - "World War Two happened because Hitler was evil". Tabloid newspapers are often said to lack nuance. Their discussion is crude, rather than subtle.

objective. A truth that is accessible generally rather than to just one particular individual or to particular individuals. Science is often said to be "objective", because it relies on experiments which can be repeated by anyone, not just that particular investigator. Opposite of **"subjective"** – subjective meaning rooted in personal opinion and in the viewpoint of the individual subject. So, your favourite flavour of ice-cream is a subjective choice. Your favourite type of music to listen to is a subjective choice. They are choices that can't really be "wrong". The word "objective" also can be used in the sense of trying to escape from the individual point of view, "Objectively speaking, it is difficult to say that West Ham are a better team than Man Utd. In my heart however, I cannot accept that they are". Nouns: objectivity, subjectivity.

orthodox. This refers to the conventionally accepted position on something. This word is probably religious in origin i.e. being used to indicate what was considered to be correct religious belief. But it can very much be used in other contexts e.g. in football a 4-4-2 formation is fairly orthodox.

heretical. The opposite of orthodox is **heretical**, linked to the word **"heresy"**.

Another relevant term here is **"revisionist"**. Revisionist historians are those who challenge the current orthodoxy. **Post-revisionists** challenge the revisionists, whose interpretation in turn might have become a new orthodoxy.

ostensible. The ostensible reason for doing something is the pretended reason for doing something. It is the *apparent* reason that it was done, but not the *real* reason that it was done.

putative. Means "supposed". The supposed reason that something was done, although there is no direct evidence of this.

paradigm. Means a perspective or a certain way of looking at things. "Viewed through this paradigm" means viewed from this fundamental perspective. You can also use the word "**optic**" here, a word that carries the implication of how you look at something (optical, optician). An even fancier word is **Weltanschauung**, German for "worldview". Using this will sound pretentious, but it might be a useful one to recognise.

paradox. Something which is true, but surprisingly so, because it contains apparently contradictory elements. So, for example, doing well in exams requires you to really make the most of your time off. This is something of a paradox! Adjective - paradoxical.

peripheral. On the margins, on the **periphery**. That was a peripheral consideration. It was not a central consideration. To see something in your peripheral vision is to see it while you are looking directly at something else. He was a peripheral figure – not at the centre, not a central figure.

persuasive. To find an argument persuasive means that you find it convincing.

pervasive. A view that is pervasive is one that is widely held.

permeate. To spread throughout. In Biology a permeable membrane is one that allows matter to pass through it.

platitude. Something that is often said, but that doesn't necessarily mean anything much. e.g. "Time is a great healer", or "The grass is always greener on the other side of the fence". Adjective – **platitudinous**.

plausible. Believable. A plausible argument is a convincing argument.

postulate. To suppose that something is true for the sake of argument. It is an idea that is claimed, provisionally, to be true. It is similar to putting forward a **hypothetical** idea (see definition above).

pragmatic. Practical. This action was taken for pragmatic reasons. The opposite of "principled". Often has **connotations** of "common sense".

connotations. To carry an implication of something. "The hesitancy of his language connoted a certain **ambivalence** on this issue". Verb – to connote.

precedent. "This behaviour on his part was not without precedent". It, or something similar, had happened, before. This is a key word in legal terminology. Judges deciding on a case in front of them will rely on the precedents provided by previous cases. It's opposite is "unprecedented".

preclude. This precludes the possibility that X. This means that X is no longer possible.

proponent. That Member of Parliament is a proponent of devolution. She argues for devolution. She **advocates** devolution.

propound. To propound an argument means to put it forward, to set it out, to promote it.

purported. Means "supposed" or "alleged" or "claimed". He is purported to have made these allegations in private. Some people are saying that he made these allegations.

qualify. To qualify an argument means to set out its limitations. By doing so you help to define what you are actually saying. So, the statement X must be qualified by the points Y and Z. Paradoxically, by pointing out the limitations of what you are saying, you actually make it tighter and stronger. By being clear that you are not saying Y or Z, it's more clear what you actually *are* saying.

qualities. Means "characteristics". Strictly speaking, this word is value-neutral. "Lancelot, while on the whole an admirable man, had a number of unappealing qualities."

raft of ideas. This useful little phrase refers to a whole stack of ideas. It Is useful when gesturing towards a pile of ideas that are in a bit of a jumble, meaning that it is difficult to refer to them more neatly. "In the meeting we had a brainstorm and came up with a raft of ideas as to how we might do things better".

ramifications. Implications. The ramifications of this speech will be enormous.

rationale. The reason for doing something. The rationale behind his change of tactics was as follows, ...XYZ.

reciprocal. An arrangement in which the same thing is going the other way. Argentina has a reciprocal extradition agreement with the United Kingdom, meaning that suspected criminals can be extradited in both directions.

unilateral. This means just going ahead and doing something on your own, without necessarily even consulting other people who might have an interest in the situation. "Karen unilaterally decided that they would all go and see the film she had chosen. She booked everyone's tickets without even asking them".

refute. To refute an argument means to demonstrate that it is incorrect.

requisite. Required. He did not have the requisite determination to succeed. He turned up to make the application, but without the requisite photographs.

rhetorical. Refers to the art of putting forward an argument, or more generally, to the making of speeches. Cicero is widely thought to have been the greatest **rhetorician** off all time.

rhetorical question. This is a question that you ask your audience but to which you will provide the answer. You ask the question as a means of putting your point more forcefully. It is the sort of question that someone skilled in the art of rhetoric might ask. Do you think this technique could be useful in essays? Well yes it can.

rhetoric. Argument. To say that something is "just rhetoric", is to suggest that it is just posturing. Politicians are often accused of just engaging in political rhetoric and point-scoring rather than dealing constructively with the issues at hand. It's a criticism, and implies that what's being said is just "hot air".

substantive. The substantive point here is XYZ. What we talking about here is the real weight of the argument, the solid argument that is being put forward here in Contrast the issue of how that particular argument is being expressed. If **rhetoric** is the packaging, the **substantive** argument is the content that lies inside the packaging.

salient. The salient point here is that... The most important point here is that. Literally means "sticking out".

specious. Illegitimate. Flawed, and possibly intentionally so. The football manager's answer on this point was specious. This means that the manager was being dishonest. The word **spurious** is broadly similar in meaning and is usually applied to arguments that you think are nonsense, and maybe involve an element of deception.

disingenuous. Dishonest. To pretend that something is the case when in fact it is not is to act disingenuously.

supposition. Something that has been supposed, or assumed. Your supposition that I was late on purpose is completely incorrect.

surrogate. Substitute for.   A surrogate mother is someone who agrees to give birth to a baby for another couple.

tautology. This is a grammatical error that involves saying the same thing twice. So, for example: the big giant. All giants are big. If you are comparing two giants it should be "the bigger giant". If you are drawing attention to one of three or more giants it should be "the biggest giant". By using the word "giant" we already know that we are talking about someone big. The adjective here is **"tautological"**. It is tautological to say that that Nazis were fascists. It is self-evident to say this. It is so obvious that the Nazis were fascists, that to say it doesn't really add anything to what we have already communicated by using the term "Nazis". (That said, it seems very likely that not all members of the Nazi Party agreed with its beliefs.") Another example here would be an expression like "Very crucial": something is either "crucial" or it's not, there are not degrees of "crucialness".

tenable. That position is not tenable. It is not sustainable. That argument doesn't hold water.

tenuous. Smith's argument here is somewhat tenuous. It is weak.   It doesn't really add up.

thesis. The argument that is being put forward.   The work people do towards a doctorate is known as their doctoral thesis.

truism. Something that is so generally accepted as being true it is hardly worth saying it. "It is a truism to say that x,y,z".

ubiquitous. Found everywhere.   This winter camel-coloured coats are ubiquitous.

veneer. Thin layer of. In the construction of furniture a veneer of more expensive wood, like oak, is often stuck on top of cheaper material. Their veneer of civility masked the brutality that lay underneath.

Useful Latin words to know

I don't particularly like the use of Latin in academic work, because it often makes it difficult to work out what someone is actually saying.

HOWEVER other people will use it quite often, so here are some key terms that you should at least recognise.

a priori . Literally means "from what comes before". In practice this is used to refer to a state of affairs that is taken for granted.

ad hominem. Literally means "to the man". An ad hominem attack is one where you attack the person saying something rather than what he's saying.

ad infinitum. Literally "to infinity". Endlessly.

ad nauseam. Literally "to sickness". Excessively. "This topic has been debated ad nauseam".

caveat emptor. Buyer beware. Buying property is caveat emptor, in the sense that if anything turns out to be wrong with it, you can't get your money back.

cogito ergo sum. "I think therefore I am". Famously said by the philosopher Descartes.

de facto. In fact. "He was the de facto leader of his country, even though no formal elections had taken place".

de jure. According to law. "After the elections had taken place he was the de jure leader of his country".

e.g. *Exempli gratia*. Meaning "for example".

ergo. Therefore.

i.e. id est. Literally means "that is". Meaning "in other words". "The current English cricket team has adopted similar tactics to those used by the strongest side of the 1990s i.e. the Australians".

ibid. Meaning "in the same place". You will often see this word in footnotes, meaning that the material in this particular footnote was drawn from the same place as that of the previous footnote.

inter alia. "Among other things". "Professor Blythe has *inter alia* contributed articles to the "The Economist" magazine"

ipso facto. Literally "by the fact itself". Means "in and of itself".

modus operandi means "way of going about things"

non sequitur. Literally "does not follow". e.g. "Given the size of the universe, there must be a moon somewhere that is in fact made of cheese". In reality this is not necessarily the case – they might just all be made of rocks!

nota bene. NB. Literally "note well". Or "Pay particular attention to the following". "NB that the Board's decision on this issue was far from unanimous".

per se. In and of itself. Intrinsically. "It is accurate to say that killing another human being is wrong *per se*?"

quid pro quo. Literally meaning "what for what". Suggests the idea of an agreement where one thing is exchanged for another.

quod erat demonstrandum. Meaning "which was to be demonstrated". Frequently used in the sense of "I have just shown / proven this".

sic. Meaning "thus". Used to suggest that a mistake is not the writer's own. "The suspect had written a note to his brother to suggest that 'tonite was definAtely the nite'" [sic] *sine qua non*. Literally "without which not". Used to describe an essential condition of something else happening. For example, creativity is the *sine qua non of art*.

status quo. The way things are. The current state of affairs.

sui generis.   Literally "of its own kind". "The solution devised was sui generis" – it applied, and could only apply, in that particular situation.

viz. Means "as follows" or "namely". "My grandfather had three sons viz Tom, Dick and Harry".

Oxbridge applications

Here are few thoughts in case you are thinking of going down this road:

Don't assume that "Oxbridge isn't for me": There are lots of different types of people at Oxbridge. The "toff" stereotypes are rarely accurate. The vast majority of people there are bright and hardworking rather than being intellectual giants. The colleges vary widely in character and it is worth doing some research into which to apply to. Have a look at the "Alternative Prospectus" written by current students.

Make use of all the resources you possibly can:

- Ask for extra help from tutors: "If you don't ask you don't get".
- Ask someone who has gone through the interview process for your subject.
- Read books on how to get into Oxbridge – they are available on Amazon.
- Your school may have reports from former pupils who have had interviews or gone to Oxbridge. They might even be willing to meet up for a chat.

You will need to do a lot of extra work: Most people at interview will already have excellent results at school and you may need something more to impress. Find out which books to read by asking your tutor, and by looking on Amazon and Google. Focus on understanding in depth, rather than on breadth. If there is something that you know about then try to get talking on that subject.

Be prepared to think: In your interview they will want to test how well you can think on the spot, and how deep your understanding of the material really is.

Some questions can be a little "wacky": In my interview for law I was asked whether I would be guilty of murder if I made a voodoo doll of my interviewers and they subsequently died from mysterious illnesses! Questions like this test whether intelligently pick an issue apart (p 90).

There are books full of questions like this, so make sure you get your hands on one and practise approaching them.

What are they looking for?   Tutors, on the whole, and with some honourable exceptions, are more interested in their own research than in teaching undergraduates.   They get annoyed by people who turn up to tutorials unprepared.   They want likeable, lively and intellectually curious characters who will work hard and who be a pleasure to teach.

Accept that there is a large element of luck involved: Yes there are some complete geniuses who are almost certain to get in, but I only met about three of them during my whole time at Oxford.   Most people have just worked hard, worked smart, and had a bit of luck.

Thanks to...

I'd like to say a very big thank-you to all my friends who have contributed towards this book, and who have supported me throughout this project. In particular I'd like to thank: Albertine Davies, Owe Carter, Helena Braun, Eleanor James, Graham Geary, Jeremy and Liz Nuttall, Matthias Oschinski, Trevor McDevitte, Sally Waples, David Smith, Paul Broom, Iain Jones, Will Wyman, Nicholas Lawn, and Kirk Huff. I'd also like to thank those friends who contributed but who preferred to remain anonymous.

I would particularly like to thank Karen Lawrence, without whose help this book would not have been written.

Thank you also (very much) to my family for their love and support. Thanks very much indeed to my Mum and Dad for all your encouragement (not to mention proof-reading the entire text!). Thanks also to Marjory Mackay and to Angus Mackay, and to the Mackenzies and the Livingstones for all your kindness and fun along the way.

Very special thanks to my lovely wife Emily who has given me so much support and encouragement throughout, and to whom this book is dedicated with my love.

Patrick

About the author

Patrick McMurray studied Law at Worcester College Oxford, followed by a Masters degree in Forced Migration in the Department of International Development at the same university. After completing the Legal Practice Course at the College of Law he worked as a solicitor in London and he has also worked in a legal capacity for the Refugee Law Project at the University of Makerere in Kampala, Uganda. One day soon he will complete a further degree in Ancient and Modern History at Queen's University Belfast. He currently lives in Paris with his wife Emily.